Are you intrigued by the mystery of

THE BERMUDA TRIANGLE?

Then consider the unsolved disappearances in the

TRIANGLE OF TERROR

What about the freighter, the **Ourand Medan?** Did a supernatural power strike out and not obliterate? What was the weird influence that made the ship's radio operator signal with such desperate finality, "I die!"?

Was the fatal force terrestrial or extraterrestrial? What horror were the terrified victims staring at when they died?

Adi-Kent Thomas Jeffrey reviews the known facts, the legends and the unsolved mysteries for you to think about!

Also by Adi-Kent Thomas Jeffrey

THE BERMUDA TRIANGLE

Published by
WARNER BOOKS

Triangle of Terror and Other Eerie Areas

by
Adi-Kent Thomas Jeffrey

WARNER BOOKS

A Warner Communications Company

WARNER BOOKS EDITION
First Printing: August, 1975

Library of Congress Catalog Card Number: 75-4989

This Warner Books Edition is published
by arrangement with New Hope Publishing Company.

Cover design by Gene Light

Cover photograph by PHOTOWORLD

Warner Books, Inc., 75 Rockefeller Plaza, New York, N.Y. 10019.

A Warner Communications Company

Printed in Canada.

Not associated with Warner Press, Inc. of Anderson, Indiana.

To Tom who loves the farthest reaches of his wondrous, snow-clad area, and so will surely be lured by regions such as these.

ACKNOWLEDGMENTS

To the many individuals and organizations in this country as well as in England, Scotland, Italy, Hungary and Russia who aided me in the research for this book, my most grateful appreciation.

CONTENTS

INTRODUCTION

The eerie areas of the world surround us more than we realize. Like the Van Allen "belt" of radiation encompassing our earth some 400 miles above and beyond, some things have been out of man's ken for ages. But not forever. Eventually they are discovered, with no little awe, by the ever-expanding curiosity of man's mind about his environment.

But many strange factors take time to surface.

Like the mysterious "Triangle" zones of the world. Researching into those puzzles for my last book, *The Bermuda Triangle*, served well to remind me more fully how much there is yet for man to unravel about the nature of his universe.

It is not surprising to find more and more Triangle Troubles, rather than less, as investigators search deeper into the "whys" and "wherefores" of our world. Mysteries usually do become more puzzling before they bow to solution, like the muddy river bed that must be stirred before it can be purified.

So, perhaps, we will be learning of more Mystery Zones around the globe all the time. It will not be just the "Bermuda Triangle" off North America and the "Devil's Sea" off Japan, but other areas where men and craft have been disappearing or confronting strange unknown conditions for many years.

Is the East Indian Ocean one of these regions?

An American organization called SITU (Society for the Investigation of the Unexplained) composed of biologists, oceanographers, geophysicists, mathematicians and other scientists active in researching the Triangle Mystery, recently came to the conclusion it is. One thing sure, the Indian Ocean has been a region of odd occurrences for centuries. You will read about some of them in the opening chapter of this book.

But this "Triangle Deadliness" is not the only oddity man is encountering in his world. There are countless other places and things that defy natural laws as we know them. Weird wastes and strange seas that arouse both fear and curiosity. They, too, are everywhere. Some are rooted and grounded into their defying mysteries, forever, it would seem. Others, like the taunting will-o'-the-wisp of the marsh-lands, make their awesome presences known for a while; then shift to establish new domains or vanish utterly.

It has been my fortune to have crossed several times over the elusive boundary that separates the earth from the unearthly.

One such occasion was the weird experience of "rolling" *uphill* on a back road, Pleasant Valley Road, in Mercer County, New Jersey (a few miles east of Lambertville). Of course, if one happens on such a freak incline, it is equally sense-boggling to turn the car around and "climb" *downhill!* Such areas are called "anti-gravity" hills. They are becoming, I am beginning to believe, as commonplace along country byways as picnic areas. I have been told of no less than five anti-gravity stretches within 20 miles of my home in Pennsylvania.

I have also had the stunning experience of entering one of those capricious, here-for-a-moment mysteries. A *patch* of rainfall. It was so small a square of concrete highway—perhaps, ten feet by ten—one could hardly define it as an area. Yet, it was there. And it was beyond all normal physics.

I had just pulled off a side road into Route 611 in Doylestown, Pennsylvania, when it occurred. On a brilliant, sunny day without a cloud in the sky and a wide highway in front of me, I suddenly saw a square of rainfall ahead! The pinpoints of precipitation were clearly visible (it was no shimmering from oil or reflections) and they started from a height of about four feet over the road, hitting the surface with a delicate splashing.

Fortunately, I was not alone. My daughter, riding with me, saw it, too. My sanity felt saved.

One is never alone in the strange events of life. All of mankind have been sharing them with each other for hundreds of years. Men have been puzzled by "rains" far weirder than the one on Highway 611. They have been pelted by seemingly sourceless snowballs, stones and even, believe it or not, flesh! But now I am giving away Chapter 10!

Suffice it to say, you have a new journey ahead of you. Before you reach the final chapter, you will have traveled through many eerie waters and winds and lands. Enjoy the adventure and, as they say to the traveler in Africa, "Go gently!"

Chapter One

Though the stem of the Maranti tree
*   rocks to and fro*
Let the Yam leaves be as thick as possible
That Rain and Tempest and all Evil
*   may come to naught!*

Malayan charm

INDIAN OCEAN—
TRIANGLE OF TERROR?

Something in the very name, "Indian Ocean," has always conjured up images of the mysterious and unknown, long before talk of Triangles of Terror came into being.

Vaporous mountains there rise from the waters. Sands and suns; feathery rain and foliage, thick as fondant, set a seductive trap. Nowhere, more than in this spot, have centuries of sea brought forth more tales of shipwreck, piracy, smuggling, drug trafficking and primitive adventure.

It seems only natural then to find this area, lusty as it is alluring and mystical as it is mysterious, the age-old setting for disastrous voyages, macabre deaths and ghostly ships. Only natural, also, for it to emerge today in a new light more inexplicable, perhaps, than any eeriness it ever emitted in the past—that new view of a "Triangle of Terror."

Whatever lies behind the odd happenings of the Indian Ocean, one thing is for sure. It is not new. Strange things have been going on there for countless years. One of the earliest known of such puzzling occurrences happened in the late 1700's. It catapulted the fabled area into widespread attention.

The name, Captain Jean-Francois de Galaup, Comte de la Pérouse, is a shadowy one, if anything at all, to the modern historian. To France of the late 18th century, he was sailor, soldier, hero, patriot, adventurer and explorer. He ended up in one more category. He topped the greats on the Missing Person List. But that was not a distinction to capture too much attention since he had the misfortune of disappearing off the surface of the sea in the year 1789 . . . the year the French Revolution broke out. Pérouse's government was not unconcerned, just unavailable. In spite of its preoccupations, though, the newly-established French National Assembly passed a decree in 1790 which read in part:

". . . orders to all ambassadors, residents, consuls, and national agents at the courts of foreign powers that they may engage those different sovereigns, in the name of humanity and of the arts and sciences, to charge all navigators and agents whatsoever, their subjects, in whatever place they may be . . . to make inquiry after the two French frigates, *La Boussole* and *L'Astrolabe,* commanded by M. de la Pérouse as well as after their crew, and to obtain every information which may ascertain their existence or their shipwreck. . ."

La Pérouse's exploratory voyage had been organized in 1785. It consisted of two frigates bearing a comprehensive party that included a geographer, civil engineer, surgeon, astronomer, physicist, botanist and even clock-maker. The group was prepared to survey, map and investigate any distant shores overlooked by earlier English, Dutch and Portuguese explorers.

Sailing bravely forth from the ancient port of Brest on August 30, 1785, the tiny fleet ran a long slant across the Atlantic to Brazil; then down around Cape Horn to the Sandwich Islands discovered by Captain Cook only a few years earlier. From there, La Pérouse pulled northward to the Alaskan coast of America, exploring glacier-locked bays and ice-packed shores.

Coasting southwards, the two frigates made their way to Monterey Bay where the Spanish missions of California welcomed them warmly.

Next, the most ambitious, La Pérouse decided to cross the unknown stretches of the Pacific. This brought him to Guam and, further on, to Manila. From there he pushed on to explore Formosa and the coast of Tartary. Setting sail once more, the weary party floated into the much needed calm of the tranquil South Seas. But a clash with natives on the Navigator Islands caused the loss and wounding of thirty-two French sailors.

Short-handed and dismayed at this turn of event, La Pérouse pulled into Botany Bay, Australia, seeking assistance from the English colony there. The exploration party had been away from France for almost three years.

Colonists lining the wharf, gazed awestruck at the straggling voyagers. The frigates' hoisted sails were patched and threadbare, so delicate of substance, it seemed a slight breeze would blow them from the yards. The men's clothing was equally shabby. The paint on the ships' sides and bulwarks was completely weatherworn and weeds and barnacles clung to the planking and railings. The decks were cracked and blistered by tropical suns.

No longer shining smartly with flags a-flutter, the two French frigates looked like phantom ships of old sailors' yarns. However, the explorer was undaunted. In a short time he was planning to sail again.

"Are your men not mutinous? Weary? Desirous of returning home?" he was asked by the island's residents.

"My men are ready for but one thing—to follow me to the ends of the earth!"

And, if there is an edge anywhere to the earth's known realms, then that is, indeed, where La Pérouse and his devoted crews must have gone.

He set sail from Botany Bay with a course planned to reach Mauritius in the Indian Ocean before the end of that year in 1788. His two ships, frail and gray in the brilliant tropical air, whisked off into the distant greens and blues of the Indian Ocean and, though successful voyagers across the seas of the whole world, there, they came to an unknown and mysterious end. They were never seen or heard from again. They became one of the world's unsolved mysteries.

But La Pérouse's disappearance is actually the least baffling of that eastern sea's challenging secrets. Consider the case of the Dutch freighter, the S.S. *Ourand Medan*. In February of 1948 the vessel was bound for Jakarta, Indonesia. On a mild, sun-filled day with a sea smooth as water-worn stone, the freighter plied effortlessly through the

Straits of Malacca between Sumatra and the Malay Peninsula. There was not a hint of trouble of any kind.

Then, without warning, Dutch and British radio posts heard SOS signals from the freighter, followed by the ship's location.

Over and over, the distress calls were repeated. Then came the distraught message:

"All officers including captain dead, lying in the chartroom and on bridge . . . probably whole crew dead." That was all, save for a few incoherent signals, until a last significant word phrase:

"I die."

Vessels in the area were quickly notified and within a few hours, the stricken ship was sighted. She seemed in perfect condition but was propelled by no power, simply drifting aimlessly with the currents.

Receiving no replies to repeated hails, the rescuing ships sent boarding parties onto the steamer.

They were speechless with horror. It was a ship of the dead. The captain was sprawled and lifeless on the bridge. The other officers lay gaunt and cold in the chartroom and the wheelhouse. Along the deck were strewn the bodies of the crew members. In the radio room, the operator who had so desperately called for help, now lay dropped in his chair, his hand resting where it had been to his last moment— on the transmitting key.

Concluding the macabre setting, are the words of the report put out later by the *Proceedings of the Merchant Marine Council*, a board who interviewed the rescuers and investigated in depth the inexplicable tragedy of the S.S. *Ourand Medan*. The report quoted witnesses as saying, "Their frozen faces were upturned to the sun. The mouths were gaping open and the eyes staring."

As the last punctuation to a startling disaster, a new mysterious element cast its shadow over the whole puzzle. Just as the boarding parties were discussing ways and means of towing the grisly cargo back to port, a fire burst forth from the ship's hold, spreading like panic. The men fled back to their own ships, just minutes before the boilers of the Dutch freighter exploded, sending the vessel reeling over and down into the depths of the Indian Ocean.

What caused the mass deaths? Disease? Not with such suddenness. Poison? Hardly, with all, including a dog, needing to partake simultaneously and no suggestion of poison symptoms from the radio operator. Lethal gas? Not likely, it had been judged, since the end comes peacefully under those conditions, not torturously. An attack by the supernormal powers? This has been suggested, too. But there was no hint of this from the radio operator, either. What then? Why the explosion? To this day no conclusion has been reached.

Only the inscrutable Indian Ocean knows the answers.

But long before either of these incredible occurrences a Dutch merchant vessel under the command of a Captain Bernard Fokke, set sail from its home port of Holland one clear day in the spring of 1650.

Though no one knew it at the time, it was to be the most famous voyage of all time.

But Captain Fokke (some versions give his name

21

as "Vanderdecken") that breeze-filled day in 1650 had no awareness of any such pending immortality. He knew only he had a hold full of cargo due at ports in the Indies and he was not a man to waste time because of rumblings amongst the townspeople. And rumblings there were, for this Friday was not a day for a ship to put to sea. It was Good Friday and no man could be bold or evil enough to dare to sail on such a sacred day, murmured the Hollanders, as they crowded about his ship at the wharf.

But Bernard was hard-cored enough to scorn such useless superstitions.

"I have my job to be doing and not Hell or high waves can keep me from it!" As he swung onto the gangway, he aimed a hearty kick at a gaping youth who had stumbled against him by chance. "Stare too hard, me lad, at me vessel and ye'll risk hanging from the yard with me hauling the rope!"

In the next instant, the captain stepped aside willingly as two sailors rolled up casks of rum and brandy.

A woman in the crowd on the dock shook her pink-cheeked face. "I tell ye," she whispered to her neighbor, "Old Fokke has himself damned this day! Sailin' on Good Friday, preparin' for carousin' on board with rum that's not marked for the Indies but for the captain!"

"Aye," answered her friend, "and for who else, only Heaven be knowing!"

"Ye speak of the tales we be hearing of the wenches he's said to take along with him on these voyages? Aye, no doubt, 'tis true. . ."

An old man behind the two women pulled a pipe out of his mouth and rasped loudly into their ears.

" 'Tis a limb of the Devil, he is! More than wenching and wining sends that man to Hell, I say. 'Tis his speed of voyage! Did you know it took him only three months to sail from Amsterdam to Batavia! No human could do it! Any seafarin' body knows that."

The women nodded until their white starched head pieces crackled. "Captain Fokke is no ordinary man. He serves the Devil, not the Dutch East India Company!"

"Bernard Fokke," shrieked out a woman at the dock's end, as the high curved merchantman eased out to sea. "Ye have sworn and blasphemed and dared to sail against the wind as only wizards are wont. But now ye have called down the angels' anger, sailing on Good Friday! Ye will not forget this day, I warrant!"

The huge Hollander laughed as he leaned over the oaken railing and spat into the waters swirling below. Then he uttered a curse that was lost on the hum of the wind. In the next few minutes the high-sterned vessel swooped airily out to sea, headed for the Indian Ocean . . . and eternity.

After that day, no sign of Captain Bernard Fokke, or of any of his crew or any rail or timber from his ship or of so much as a button or a rag of sail was ever seen by anyone again.

His vessel never arrived at the designated ports. No word as to his whereabouts was ever gleaned from any of the trading ships who plied the heavily-trafficked route from western ports to Indonesia.

Captain Bernard Fokke, as his fellow Hollanders had so vehemently predicted, left this earth on that sacrilegious voyage for good!

Or did he?

Within a year of the disappearance of Amsterdam's wild and wilful blasphemer, a merchantman returning to port from the Indies, arrived with a startling story. Its captain and crew said that they had seen Fokke's vessel whilst they were laboring in a storm in the Indian Ocean. It had been clearly in sight, in spite of high waves and violent flashes of lightning that battered and wrenched the pale hulk. The merchantman decided to make an approach as near as possible and see if a rescue could be effected. The crew, clinging to fore-and-aft rails, called to each other, even though the wind smothered their cries with its powerful force.

" 'Tis Fokke himself! See how he stands on the quarter deck, awash with waves, as though he'd beat the lightning with a single fist!"

"Aye, and look at his men! Gaunt enough they appear as though not biscuit or grog has passed their lips in months!"

By now the merchantman hove close enough to bespeak. The captain raised his brass trumpet and shouted a hail. In the next instant, to the astonishment of the captain and crew, the heaving, riddled ship with its worn-faced seamen, vanished. There was nothing athwart now but rolling sea and empty winds!

The Hollanders nodded their heads. " 'Twas old Fokke himself, for sure, sailing the orders of the Devil."

24

Over the following months, the vessel was reported as being sighted several times in the Indies. The accounts ran similar. She was always spotted at a distance in a storm or a mist. Through a spy glass and the far-seeing eye of the sailor aloft, she was described as obviously in distress. When the sighting vessel would hove close enough to see in detail, the scene was always the same—a gray, bearded captain scanning the seas; a crew of wild-eyed seamen desperately calling for assistance. Then just as the rescuing ship would get within hailing distance, the *Flying Dutchman*, as she was already called, would disappear.

The seventeenth century was filled with sightings of the condemned ship. Then as new centuries bore down, new routes for the ornery Dutchman became part of the pattern. All through the eighteenth and nineteenth centuries, stories of seeing the specter ship became legion. They formed the main conversation of tavern talk and quarter deck recountings all over the world.

Is there any substance to any of the tales worth considering?

Well, here is an incident described by the captain of a British ship that occurred only nine years before the advent of the twentieth century. It happened in an era when even ghost ships were of modern variety . . . nineteenth century clippers or steamers or men-o-war vessels with the only unreal characteristics being lights in the rigging and on deck, or phosphorescent hulls. But listen to this story from the year 1891 from a very pragmatic British skipper.

Lifting out of a gray sea-mist on a breath-still night loomed a sight that caught the attention of every man aboard the English ship. They strained all eyes and picked out the eerie outlines of a vessel such as no man there had ever seen before. In the words of the captain she was:

". . . painted a pale yellow. Her bows were low in the water and her stern high. It was crowned by a sort of double poop, one being built above the other. From what I could see of the stern, it was shaped somewhat like a pear, if you can imagine one turned upside down with the narrow end cut off. The ship had three masts, the top sections being tall and circular, like towers, with sails of fine texture hanging from the yards."

A perfect description, though with some mystical overtones, of a Dutch merchantman of the seventeenth century whose stern was uniquely shaped like an upturned pear with the slim end squared off! Quite a detailed description to be recounted by a modern-era crew who claimed no knowledge of the merchant ships of centuries earlier.

The *Flying Dutchman*, if thousands of sightings over several centuries are to be believed, sails eternally.

Does Bernard Fokke get his mysterious reappearing powers from some strange force or influence peculiar to the place of his ghost-ship's inception, the Indian Ocean?

If one examines the theories relating to the Triangle Mystery phenomenon, one might believe that such is the case. The late Ivan Sanderson, scientist, editor and lecturer, devoted much of his later life to investigating the Triangle puzzle. Such weird circumstances came into play, he believed, where vortices exist—the flowing of warm water into cold or vice versa. Perhaps, he suggested, since such whirlpools exist on earth's surface, other forces in the atmosphere, such as a new type of gravity unknown to us at the present time, are present and conform in pattern to the vortices of the seas. Their power might act to suck up or transplant men and ships that come within their spheres of influence. We can't be sure how many such Triangle areas exist, but from the statistics investigators have been accumulating, they certainly appear to be existent in the Indian Ocean, both to the southwest and to the far east as well as in the Bermuda zone and the area south of Japan.

Looking back over some of the inexplicable events of the Indian Ocean region, was there a strange force that swept Bernard Fokke and his ship off the ocean; then "replayed" the event like a visual and auditory "record" for subsequent generations?

Did that same force remove the explorer La Pérouse and his fleet in the 18th century?

And what about the freighter, the *Ourand Medan*? Did that supernatural power in that case simply strike out and not obliterate? What was the weird influence that made that ship's radio operator signal so surely and desperately, "I die."?

Was the force terrestrial or extra-terrestrial? What were the frightful-faced victims, including the dog, staring at when they died? Many UFO theorists declare they were visited by outer space beings. Such intelligences could prefer the vortice areas as their source of material when they wish samples of men and machines to take back to their home planets.

Or are the forces felt by man in unique areas of the world related not to whirlpools or extra-terrestrial beings at all but to some strange property of electromagnetic forces that we are not yet familiar with? Many scientists today are searching this realm for a possible key to the puzzle.

No one has a definite conclusion yet. Only speculations. Thousands of interested people are watching the investigators, waiting for the answer, shaking their heads meanwhile over what is surely the most engrossing new puzzle of our earth—the Triangle phenomenon.

Chapter Two

9:52   *Our mainmast by the board . . . Few of our men left.*
10:15   *Most of our men are dead.*

> Last entry in ship's log, November 1814, of American sloop-of-war. Found at turn of the century by the stranded victim, Elisha Thompson, on derelict warship in the Sargasso.

DEADLY SARGASSO

Some investigators into the troubling Triangle Mystery feel that the Bermuda zone extends beyond the cluster of islands into the south mid-Atlantic.

If they are right, then an area of ocean that plagued man for centuries is part of the famous "Bermuda Triangle." With its ancient reputation for "deadliness," one can hardly deny it belongs there, for the mysterious region has long been called in fact and legend, the "Deadly Sargasso."

The Sargasso Sea pinpoints on the map at 20° and 35° north latitude and 30° and 70° west longitude. For early seafaring man it pinpointed horror. That weed-choked area of the Atlantic sparked fear and imagination from the first time it was sighted by an adventurer's eyes. That adventurer was Christopher Columbus.

On September 16th of 1492 during his historic voyage to the New World, Columbus' fleet was becalmed in the Sargasso Sea.

Upon his return home, the explorer told his fellowmen of the awesome ocean region.

"When I came a hundred leagues west of the

Azores," he informed the world, "I noticed an extraordinary change in the aspect of the sky and the stars, in the temperature of the air and in that of the sea. I found the surface of the water covered so thickly with vegetation resembling small branches of fir that we believed we must be in shallow waters and that the ships would soon be aground for lack of depth."

It was weeks before the *Santa Maria*, the *Pinta* and the *Nina* were free of the snare of tangling, yellow and green seaweed. The terrifying entrapment the great navigator and his men went through struck fear into the stoutest of voyagers everywhere for centuries afterward.

All through the eras of ever-wider navigation that followed Columbus' voyage, tales circulated in seafront taverns and cabin boys' quarters of the frightful Sargasso. Gold-heavy galleons, war-torn frigates and rich-laden merchantmen, it was reported, had sailed into the giant grasp of tentacled seaweed, never to escape. Survivors of derelict clipper ships and even steamers of the later years, told of the unbelievable sight of drifting, helpless ships caught into a solid knot of wreckage. Some of them were abandoned; others afloat with a cargo of skeletons.

The fearful accounts caught on with a tenacity as stubborn as the clutching of the Sargasso weeds themselves. Poems, novels, word-of-mouth tales enveloped the near-legendary sea which kept alive the Sargasso's past even into this age of moon-walkers.

Today, in an era of fast mechanized ships, it is difficult to believe that any craft could be held fast by seaweed, no matter how thick-growing, but yesteryear when winds were the force that moved vessels, it was a different matter.

To deny the Sargasso its past notoriety, is blindly to discount all the many records left posterity by countless voyagers in that "Deadly Sea"; seafarers who wrote of their ordeals there with horror and sincerity.

Believer or non-believer, the Sargasso is still an unearthly sea of windless, motionless eeriness caught amongst clockwise ocean currents that still has the power to compose legends and tales for the eager listener.

One of the finest and most-stirring of these experiences is that told by an orphan boy long ago.

Elisha Thompson was a young boy without kith or kin who signed up as a cabin boy on the cargo vessel, the *J. G. Norwood* around the year 1900. The ship had been plying the seven seas of the world for over a quarter of a century. This voyage it unloaded a cargo of cotton at Galveston, Texas; then set sail for Europe with the young Elisha on board.

About three weeks later, the cargo ship ran headlong into a storm. Half a dozen of the crew and the captain were washed overboard with one overpowering wave which struck across the deck like a great hand dealing a smashing blow. In seconds, more than half the vessel's crew had been wiped away and the ship's foremast splintered with a thunderous roar.

Elisha kept a frantic eye on the two remaining crew members who were fighting to keep the storm from tearing them, too, into its whirling depths. The battle was useless. With a booming wail, the main topmast snapped and crashed to the deck, killing the two sailors.

The cabin boy, alone, was alive to continue to the end of the last voyage of the old *Norwood*.

It was a listless meandering. Drifting into the arms of one current, then into another, the embattled ship glided across the ocean's surface like a dazed and wounded warrior. There was never a soul or a ship in sight to offer the boy any hope.

Then one lonely dawn, the youth arose, once again to stare into infinity around him. He'd been adrift countless days and the despair was mounting. Provisions of food and water from the galley were plentiful. Still, unless something happened eventually, he, too, would be gone.

He narrowed his eyes and stared into the void ahead. Then he blinked. Something about the ocean was different. It was not rolling and white-capped, but still. So very still. It was not blue tipped with froth, but green. Dull green. And thick. He leaned over the oaken railing and studied the water. It looked less like ocean and more like meadow!

Then it struck. His head snapped upward as he sniffed the dank, odorous air. The Sargasso Sea! He had drifted into the dreaded ocean graveyard! Countless miles of buried depths for hundreds of missing ships for centuries!

The sight of it, alone on the derelict deck of the stricken cargo vessel, seemed to numb the heart of the solitary boy.

How could he ever be saved now? The many tales he'd heard in the darkness of the crew's quarters, dappled by the swaying glow of an overhead oil lamp, all came back to him now. They leapt to life in his frightened brain. Stilled ships caught in entangling growth that crept over their sides, crawled into cabins and passageways until they overwhelmed men in their grasp, as well as fallen masts and splintered rails and barrels and all else that crossed their paths.

Men that avoided the octopus-like weeds themselves were stifled out of life by the airless, foul-odored atmosphere—or starved to death, trapped in their floating dungeons.

Elisha Thompson ate a troubled dinner that night as he could feel the ship working its fateful way into the morass of sea growth. He lay down later, watching through a tiny porthole the moon slither ominously over the wasteland of sky.

Where would it all end for him?

The next morning he decided the best thing to do was not wait for anything to come to him. Not even death. He would go to it. Action. Action would have to prove itself the greatest value, if only to keep his mind and body alive.

The youth surveyed the scene about him that early morning. The *Norwood* had nosed its way into a mass of wreckage. Before him were crushed hulks, crazy-angled masts and pieces of ships' timbers, tumbled together into a hasty pudding. Far ahead he could see the remains of a steamer, floating evenly like a dead body on swamp waters. Beyond it were the derelict remnants of a wooden ship, water-soaked. Everywhere were piled up remains of nearly every kind of craft that ever sailed the seven seas.

Elisha swallowed, gripped firmly onto the lunch sandwiches he'd made for himself and packed into a bundle, then made a leap off the *Norwood* onto the wreck just beyond the dipping bow of his ship. Crossing from one vessel to the next one, the boy made his way from deck to deck, checking everything as he went.

The exploration soon stirred his heart with the sheer excitement of it. As he identified one ship after another, a mystery was solved! Here was this missing ship and there was that!

The blood pounded in his veins. What a hero he would be to the world to announce where this merchantman was or that long-vanished brig or such-and-such-a forgotten schooner!

He looked up and studied the worn name on the side of a rust-encrusted steamer rocking listlessly in front of him.

City of Boston! Why, that great iron steamer's disappearance had been the talk of waterfront wharves for years and years! He'd heard tell of it from many an oldtime sailor. Big iron-clad ship that was queen of the steamers from Civil War years on! Then one fine day, 'round 1870, it chugged out of New York's harbor headed for Liverpool, England, loaded with over a hundred passengers and tons of costly cargo. It was never heard from again.

And here it was!

Elisha walked along its decks with a feeling of fear hushing his own heartbeat. But there was no response to his footfalls crackling eerily over rotting boards. Then, suddenly, there was! A curious sea bird winged into sight, circled curiously about the

35

decaying ship, then flapped its wings violently and was gone.

The youth watched the creature with startled eyes until it was out of sight. Though the appearance of the bird made his skin tighten with the bleakness of it all, there was comfort to it also. Another creature in this snuffed-out world was alive besides himself!

Elisha polished off his lunch, tossed the crumbs to a cluster of crabs crawling the length of some seaweed nearby and continued his investigation of the "graveyard" of ships.

He hop-scotched across a sloop, dipping precariously on one water-logged side; swung onto the decks of a sloop-of-war and even went so far as to search the captain's quarters there, reading avidly the officer's final entry:

"The enemy sinking. We cannot help him. Most of our men are dead. All of us living are badly hurt."

Apparently after its final battle, the American war ship, with all aboard dead, had floated into the Sargasso Sea for eternal drifting.

Only skeletons stretched in dried bones on rotted hammocks and watersoaked decks were left to tell the tale to young Thompson. He swallowed hard and left the ship abruptly.

He liked his next stop the best. It was a Spanish galleon. The curve of the bottom, the majestic wooden sides swooping skyward brought to his mind the fascinating tales of plunder and glory he'd heard from so many old seamen. He hurried his now-weary legs down into the hold. Dare he expect—

He could. It was there. A king's ransom in gold, jewels and silver, still aglow, though caked with rank mold. Elisha dropped to his knees and fingered the brimful wooden chests with excitement he hadn't imagined would ever be his again.

Then the cabin boy got to his feet. He had to survive! He had to make his way back to the world and tell all he'd seen and all the riches that were now his!

With feverish action, the boy made his way back to the *Norwood*. It was dark before he made "home." He fell asleep, exhausted, but trying desperately to think of a plan for escape until the last moment of oblivion.

The plan was not soon in coming. Elisha Thompson was locked in the Sargasso for many months before he could devise a workable scheme. But devise it, he did. From this vessel and that, he painstakingly collected the necessary material. A compass from a rotting schooner and a lifeboat with a small sail from another derelict gave him highest hopes. With patient preparation, he supplied his tiny ship with ample storage of drinking water, biscuit and wine. Then he waited.

Time became hard to keep track of, but after what seemed endless weeks a fine morning dawned in which a slight breeze ruffled the tangle of curls on his head and even set some loose tentacles of seaweed wafting back and forth.

This was it! Elisha eagerly hoisted the sail. The

current of air caught it gently. Slowly, the little craft began drifting. Finally it sailed out of the rim of the Sargasso and Elisha found himself moving gradually into the glassy Atlantic.

About three weeks later, the boy found his prayers answered. He sighted a steamer on the horizon! Fortunately, the vessel saw the lifeboat, changed course and in an hour's time was hauling the weary youth on board.

The young man told his story to his rescuers and, later, recuperating in Liverpool, England, he wrote down his adventures for posterity to read.

That was to be the only and brief satisfaction he was to have. Elisha Thompson fell seriously ill shortly after his return to civilization. He died without making a scratch on the rolls of the world's brave explorers.

One more sad tale lying deep in the relentless grasp of the ancient Sargasso.

Chapter Three

The desert is the haunt of mystery. Sometimes
men hear whispers of its past.

Paul Wilhelm's Column, California,
The Indio Date Palm, October 4, 1951

LOST SHIP IN THE DESERT

One of the most alluring tales in the United States is the old and persistent rumor that somewhere in the arid sands of its Southwest a ship—perhaps several—lie buried.

Is it pure legend? Or could it be fact?

For years, reporters, travelers and historians have been trying to ascertain once and for all if there does, indeed, as legend has dictated, exist a "Lost Ship in the Desert." They are still trying.

The strange story of an earth-stranded vessel was born centuries ago around Indian campfires; then nurtured into a meaty mystery by the firesides of early pioneers. The locale has always been roughly the same: the sandy stretches north of the Mexican border and south of the Salton Sea.

This inland sea was created in the early 1900's when the waters of the Colorado River overflowed in a flood and poured into the Salton Sink, a depressed area whose history goes back to prehistoric times. A history filled with many upheavals and changes, leaving the Sink hundreds of feet below sea level. Today, the Sea occupies the lower levels of the Sink, but prior to the early 1900's, the Salton Sink stood waterless, filled only temporarily by flood waters which came and went.

Investigators into the Lost Ship lore reason, that with so many changes in topography, it is not illogical to assume that there were times in centuries past when the sea that was formed here was much larger than the present. Then the land lying between it and the head of the Gulf would have been much narrower. In that case, it would be most possible for a ship in some great Gulf storm to be swept into the lake on a powerful tidal wave. When the water eventually evaporated, the vessel would be stranded. Stranded for all eternity, as shifting sands covered and buried or dismantled and exposed it like opening the grave over whitened bones of some ancient creature.

The first stories of a strange ship were told by the Indian tribes of the Southwest. They linger on in tribal tradition. An oldtime explorer of California, Herman Ehrenberg, in the last century interviewed the chief of a Cahuilla tribe in California. The Indian described an historic incident that had been passed onto him by his father who, in turn, had received it from his father and so on. To be a good chief, explained the Indian leader, a man must be able to tell his tribe the stories of the many chiefs before him. Such recitals sometimes took days.

The chief's name was "Cabazon." Cabazon related that some three hundred years before, two ships sailed into the sea of the Salton Sink. White men in strange clothing came off the vessel and raided the nearby mountains of timber. But the local Indians

41

attacked the pale-faced boatmen and killed them. The women on board were captured and eventually sold to a tribe in western Arizona.

The tale was an old familiar one in tribal lore, asserted Cabazon.

Fascinated, Ehrenberg persisted in his search for the truth. He spent years investigating every aspect of the story. Finally, with great satisfaction, he found a tribe in western Arizona whose members had red hair and blue eyes, a fact that had existed since earliest days, long before the white men came west.

That surely must be a clue!, reasoned Herman Ehrenberg. He studied the recorded sailing history of every ship that had ever pushed into the California Gulf or up the Colorado from the Pacific. He came to the conclusion that three ships bearing a group of exiles from Europe centuries before, had reached the Pacific and thence sailed up the Colorado where a storm swept one of them into the Salton Sink. There the stranded men were killed and the women carried into captivity. Redheaded women, for sure! All of whom were sold to an Arizona tribe where they eventually became absorbed into the family life.

Ehrenberg's theory was corroborated about thirty years ago in a book written by D. and M. R. Coolidge entitled, *Last of the Seris*. The authors related the tribal tradition of the Seri Indians, a diminishing tribe who live on Tiburon Island in the Gulf of California.

"Long ago," the Indians told the authors, "when

God was a boy the 'Come-From-Afar Men' came."
Then they went on to relate how the men were tall
with white hair and beards and their women were
creamy-faced with blonde or red hair. The ship they
came in was a "long boat with a head like a snake."

The white men spent many days catching and
killing whales in the Gulf, then stripping and cooking the meat over the fires on the shores. From the
island reeds, the women fashioned baskets in which
they packed the meat. When a good supply had
been laid up, the group returned to their ship and
made sail down the Gulf. It wasn't long, however,
before the vessel ran aground and was slashed apart
by huge waves. The survivors who made it back to
shore were treated with utmost friendliness. Eventually, they married into the Indian tribe, bearing fair-
haired and blue-eyed children . . . a characteristic
of the Seris to this day.

How pleased Herman Ehrenberg would be with
such findings! However, long before this 19th century explorer had launched into his quest, the story of
a Lost Ship was going the rounds of pioneer cabins
and the blazing campfires of old prospectors, setting
into motion a whirlwind reaction.

All through the late 1860's there was a wave of
search parties outfitting themselves for long and determined desert hunts. Every time some Frontier
newspaper reported a fresh sighting of the ancient
ship, new expeditions burgeoned overnight and
ploughed expectantly through the sandy dunes for
weeks to come.

Usually those weeks proved fruitless. But not al-

43

ways. In nearly every report there was a hint of success—a clue to nurture further the story of the buried vessel.

The following article appeared in the *Los Angeles News* in September of 1870:

INTERESTING DISCOVERY

By many it has been held as a theory that the Yuma desert was once an ocean bed. At intervals, pools of salt water have stood for a while in the midst of the surrounding waste of sand, disappearing only to rise again in the same, or other localities. A short time since, one of these saline lakes disappeared and a party of Indians reported the discovery of a "big ship" left by receding waters. A party of Americans at once proceeded to the spot and found imbedded in the sands the wreck of a large vessel. Nearly one-third of the forward part of the ship, or barque, is plainly visible. The stump of the bowsprit remains and portions of the timbers of teak are perfect. The wreck is located 40 miles north of the San Bernardino and Ft. Yuma road, and 30 miles west of Dos Palmos, a well known watering place in the desert. . . .

In December of that same year, the *San Bernardino Guardian* came out with more news on the subject:

THE SEARCH FOR THE LOST SHIP

For years there have been rumors of a ship

being found upon the desert 40 to 50 miles in a southwest direction from Dos Palmos station, between San Bernardino and La Paz, and a few weeks ago Mssrs. Clicker, Caldwell and Johnson started from San Bernardino to verify the fact.

Passing south of Martinez toward the Lake they found themselves in a morass and that it was impossible to proceed further. . . . Charley Clusker organized another party of himself and Messrs. Hubble, Ferster and West, and with a four horse team came to Martinez and deflecting farther to the south crossed within a short distance of the old Ft. Yuma road, but owing to absence of fresh water were compelled to return—not, however, until Charley became convinced that he saw the ship far out in the lake. . . .

The paper goes on to report:

The indefatigable Charlie rested a day or two in San Bernardino and organized another expedition composed of J. A. Talbott, one of the editors of this paper, D. S. Ferster and F. J. West.

We had water capacity for 108 gallons, provisions for two months and four good horses and wagons . . . (wrote the paper's editor)

We came this time by a difficult route—that of the old Ft. Yuma road via Warner's Ranch and Cariso Creek station . . . here filling up our casks with water we boldly plunged out into the desert, intending to go as far as our water would permit and sending the wagon back for a fresh supply if we failed to find it. . . .

After about 20 days my business required my return, and taking two of the horses, with Ferster we crossed the intervening space between the Laguna and Martinez station, a distance of about 60 miles. The next day Ferster returned to the wagon, and we came home on one of Gus Knight's wagons, glad to see San Bernardino once more. We left the boys in good spirits, confident they will find the ship. . . .

But such hopes proved to be in vain. The same paper on January 14, 1871 published the following brief item:

RETURN OF THE SHIP PROSPECTORS
On Tuesday evening last, Charley Clusker and party returned to town, we are sorry to say, unsuccessful. . . .

Another *Guardian* recounting of 1870 serves to show the dogged determination and unquenchable fire of such explorers:

The party which left town some weeks ago for the purpose of examining the hull of a vessel said to be stranded in the Colorado Desert, has returned. All of the members of the expedition are highly pleased with the result. Though they found no ship nor any sign

46

thereof, yet they seem fully persuaded of the existence of some vessel.

Even greater persuasion was yet to come. About a quarter of a century later, a pioneer named O. J. Fisk was prospecting and mining in the Julian Banner district of San Diego County when he met an old Cahuilla Indian named Harry Chee. The elderly Indian told Fisk about the location of some gold north of Banner which sounded like good prospecting to the white man. Fisk promptly bought supplies and the two set out. They edged along the east face of the mountains until they reached a point just west of Borrego settlement.

After a day of digging the two men sat around a fire, cooking their evening meal and watching the shadows fall slowly over the surrounding sandy stretches.

Harry Chee suddenly narrowed his eyes.

"A white bird came down here once," he murmured.

Fisk stopped chewing a moment. "A white bird?"

"A big white bird, large as a hilltop!" The Indian spread his hands in a wide arc about himself. "My grandfather and his grandfather and his before him passed on the tale to us."

"Tell me, Harry, just what did this bird look like?"

The Indian turned towards him with quiet eyes.

"It brought white men to our land for the first time. It stayed with them for years. Then the bird's wings fell down and the sand covered it up."

Fish nodded and went on chewing. A strange

tale, he thought. Then he forgot about it. Until a few years later when he ran into another prospector from the Harquehala district.

"I tell you friend, I ain't never had such a diggin' day in my life! Just came from the ole Salton Sink area and didn't find no gold but a whale of a sight, all the same!"

The man's eyes seemed to burn with the recollection of an awesome thing. It reminded Fisk of Harry Chee's look that long ago evening.

"What did you see?" asked Fisk, though he was sure of the answer.

"Found me a ship, that's what! A ship in the desert! 'Course, not much left what with the shiftin' and blowin' sands. But it's there all the same. Half stickin' up outa the sand like a wounded bird, its neck all sorta carved and fancy."

Fisk nearly jumped with the suddenness of an idea.

"Tell you what, friend. Let's you and me go find that ship. Where'd you say you saw it?"

" 'Bout south end of the Sink, near to Kane Springs, guess you'd say."

"Good, I'll get back to you in short order. We'll pack a month's supplies and take off. What d'ya say, pardner?"

The two men shook hands. Sounded like adventure of the first order. But once again, a Lost Ship expedition was to end with that ever-pursuing frustration that always seemed to arise on the eve of discovery. A fierce storm arose and the wild Colorado overflowed turning the Salton Sink into the Salton Sea. O. J. Fisk was never able to make the journey.

But that doggedly determined pioneer spent much of the rest of his days trying to track down the vanished vessel legend. He liked what he finally came up with. His theory has survived the intervening decades as being one of the most logical.

Fisk learned from early Spanish writings that a flood occurred in the Colorado desert in the first half of the sixteenth century, creating a lake in the Sink of much more minor proportions than the present Salton Sea. Later, it evaporated.

The researcher found further an old account of an early seventeenth century expedition of five ships going up the Gulf of California on a pearl fishing trip from which only four returned. The fleet met a Gulf storm separating the ships from each other and forcing them to make their separate ways back to port. The missing ship was commanded by a Juan Iturbe.

Long afterwards, Iturbe showed up at Acapulco. He no longer had a ship but he had one of the world's strangest tales. His pearler, he reported, in the fury of the storm, had been blown into a narrow passage northwards which ended up in a lake. He sailed around the body of water several times, trying to find the way out. To his amazement he discovered the point of entry was gone. There was no longer a passageway into or out of the inland sea! Finally, he and his men had to abandon ship and make their way back to Mexico on foot.

Iturbe's listeners turned a doubting back to his story. More likely, they decided, he had lost his ship to pirates and feared punishment from his government for failure to resist successfully!

But, reasoned Fisk, he could have been telling the truth. Periodic river flooding had caused temporary seas in the Salton Sink, much as it had just done. Iturbe's lake could have been present in the 1600's and vanished from evaporation later on, leaving his ship sand-tied.

Fisk's final conclusion? Iturbe's ship was the Indian's "White Bird" and the old prospector's "half-stickin'-outa-the-sand" unforgettable find.

A more interesting theory was to develop as the result of another man's adventure around 1898. His name was Jesus Almanerez, a young Santa Rosa Indian from the Juarez Mountains of Lower California. He was a woodchopper who worked largely for timber, oil and mining companies.

One day in the late 1800's he was chopping wood with a crew for the Yuha Oil Well Company which was being drilled at the time. Their timber camp was located just off the Laguna Salada. Jesus and the other men cut the wood, then placed it on mules which one of them would take back to the end of the sand hills. There a wagon waited to haul the load to the oil well in the Yuha Badlands.

August came. And with it the west wind began to blow. For twelve days it blew; then came an intense rain. For days the men huddled by cabin fires until provisions were down to almost nothing.

Jesus decided to go for fresh supplies, storm or no storm. He loaded up a ten-mule train with wood and started out.

The trail pushed along the foothills but the going became too slippery to navigate. So the Indian led his pack mules off into the sand hills which were much easier going in the downpour.

He hadn't gone many miles, with a driving rain beating into his face, when he saw his lead mule stop abruptly. The animal's ears pointed sharply. The Indian raised his eyes and almost lost his breath in surprise. A huge canoe lay half buried in the side of a sand hill! It had a long neck which rose into the features of some kind of beast. Along the sides of the vessel hung round copper plates against which the rain now thrummed eerily.

Jesus Almanerez began to tremble. Men in his tribe long before him had seen such a sight. It was an evil portent. No Indian dared linger before such an evil sign. The young man slapped the mules the rest of the way as fast as he could drive them. Once at the wagon station he unloaded the wood; gathered fresh provisions and returned along the foothill trail to camp. There he drew his pay immediately and took off for the mountains. He never returned.

It was long years before Jesus ever told anyone of his frightening experience. But when he did in the early 1900's, it set off a chain of new theories. A canoe! With copper plates! Had the young Indian seen, not a Spanish galleon, but a ship of much older vintage? Was the Lost Ship a Viking vessel?

Modern historians argue that such a ship could possibly have reached there. In the tenth and eleventh centuries the northern hemisphere went through a warm era—the second following its last ice age. During this time the Arctic ice so melted that sailing ships could have gotten through, north of Canada, in what is called the Northwest Passage, where the prevailing winds came from the East. From thence they could have moved down the Pacific coast and sailed up the Colorado River. Once again, at flood time, such a ship could have been washed into the Salton Sink.

Some Indian tribes substantiate this theory with accounts of white men with red beards coming in "metal shirts" with spears and axes. Distinct descriptions of the Viking warriors.

From pirate Northmen to far-voyaging Chinese is an easy step for legend and a Colorado newspaper man in 1880 made the leap. His name was Orth Stein and he knew a good story when he found one. Like the tale of the stranded ship of Leadville. It still stands today as one of the West's most intriguing stories.

Two prospectors related the remarkable incident to Stein, he claimed, and he passed it on to the eager public in his popular *Leadville Chronicle*. It was one of his first pieces of editorship after arriving at that active silver mine camp and it was one of his best.

The men's names were Jacob Cahee and Louis Adams, prospectors for Denver, Leadville and southern Colorado speculators. They had been digging a shaft in a remote area near Red Cliff, they told Stein, when they suddenly hit a hollow sound. They tied themselves to the top of the shaft with ropes. The next thing they knew the earth gave way and they found themselves swinging suspended over a large cave.

Slowly they let themselves down and looked around. With miners' lamps they explored every part of the rock walls and sandy floor. At first, they thought the cave was empty but on closer examination, they saw a huge object at one end. As they drew nearer to it, they were astonished to see it was a sailing craft of some kind! Measuring, they estimated, about sixty feet long and thirty feet wide, it lay at a forward angle over a pile of stones. The wooden sides of the vessel seemed to be made of some dark wood like walnut. The hand-cut octagonal headed nails used for the planking were made of hard copper. They were only slightly rusty. Along the upper edge of the ship, eleven large copper rings glared back at them, probably used for securing the rigging, they reasoned.

The whole ship appeared intact but ready to crumble at the merest touch. The two men decided not to venture inside.

Lying on the floor, the prospectors found a crude instrument that resembled a sextant. The only other significant clue was discovered at one end of the ship . . . some kind of writing characters made of copper riveted onto the wood. To the gaping men, the lettering looked like Chinese hieroglyphics!

Finally, the two prospectors pulled themselves back up the shaft and made their excited way to the nearest cabin. They found it to be owned by a prosperous miner. In short order, the miner was on the way back to the underground cave with the others, eager to see the strange sight. He was not disappointed. The ship, just as the men described it, was still there.

The three decided to conceal the entrance to the hidden mystery, so that no other men might come upon it, until they were ready to disclose their find to the world. Should there be any treasure still concealed in the hold of the ancient vessel, they wanted to make sure it would be theirs. The wealthy miner promised to use all the power he possessed to protect their rights.

There was only one difficulty with the future plan. It forgot to take in the possibility that no one —not even the three men—could find the hidden entrance again! Which is exactly what happened, as so often does, with buried treasure.

Whatever the readers' opinions, Orth Stein had his own. He concluded his newspaper account with a ringing piece of prose in regards to a possible explanation for a ship becoming caught in a Colorado mountain cave:

> ". . . ages and eons, perhaps, agone, a vessel bearing a crew of bold adventurers tossed by the waves, then receding, left it stranded there. The awful upheavals and convulsions of nature, which we know so little of and can only be speculated upon, pressed the face of the earth together and sealed it in a living grave. And this is but a groping guess, yet in what strange old seas the vessel sailed, what unknown, ancient waters pressed against its peaked prow, under what prehistoric skies it pitched, what man can tell?"

Whatever the answer is to all the strange visions of ships trapped in the timeless sands of the far West, one thing is certain . . . the mystery goes on.

It has beckoned the curious for years and years. And the sightings continue. Some as recent as the 1930's.

I'm sure we can expect more.

Chapter Four

The dew drops sparkled on the rippling grass
And new-born sunbeams brightly lighted up
The Azure sky now goldly glowing from above,
As o'er him shone the fairy world of Déli Báb.

"Yanosh, the Hero" written in 1843 by
Hungarian poet, Alexander Petöfy

FATA MORGANA AND DELI BAB

The mirage. What a miracle. Even though science explains the phenomenon with ease, yet it remains an awesome show when one comes face to fabulous face with it, no matter what.

Travelers on the desert, idling ships at sea, weary wanderers on the plain . . . all of them have, for centuries, looked upward on occasion and seen the mystifying magic of a vision ahead of them in the sky.

Such vivid pictures formed in the heavens are due to an optical illusion. Under certain atmospheric conditions, a layer of air acts as a kind of mirror, casting upwards the rays of light that hit it at a grazing angle.

A very common type of mirage is the "pool" of water one often sees on the highway before him, which vanishes as the car approaches. This same effect of a body of water is often seen on a desert—always ahead and always disappearing as one moves towards it. Essentially, the "pool of water" is merely the reflection of the sky caused by the atmospheric mirror.

Sometimes this upward-cast vision is the reflection of an object far away over the horizon. A not uncommon instance of such a "looming mirage" is the ship seen "just somewhat distant" and apparently reachable in a short matter of time. It never is. As the approaching ship moves closer, the image slips away. There are numerous cases of sinking ships with screaming victims sighted by vessels at sea; yet when the rescuers hurry to their aid, the distressed ship vanishes. Actually, a ship *is* going down, just as the viewers see it. But it is not a short distance away. It is happening far away. It is just that the rays of light from that vessel have shot upwards from below the horizon and been bent back earthwards by the atmospheric mirror. Sometimes such an image appears not only closer but larger than it actually is due to not only reflection but to the magnifying qualities of the atmosphere.

Interesting as such visions are, there are even more amazing ones; the rare and beautiful "complex mirage." In these unusual circumstances, not just water or a single object but a *whole scene* is reflected in the sky. Fortunately for the world, there are two such magnificent mirages on earth. Known as "Fata Morgana" and "Déli Báb," they are considered two of Europe's most magnificent marvels.

Fata Morgana is to be found over the Strait of Messina in southern Italy. For centuries, from time to time, the atmosphere over that particular area becomes just right for casting upwards a widespread reflection in the sky. In the scene appear ships floating in the blue with men moving rhythmically at their chores on deck. Nearby a village rises from a rim of land dotted with chalk-white houses and along the shoreline caves yawn from out of mossy banks. Women are drawing water from wells; men are bent over their fishing nets. This sight captures a whole moment of a seaside village in action with its day's activities.

Not understanding the scientific reasons for such a reflection of a seaside village, the peoples of Italy in the long ago imagined it to be the work of a magician. They found just the right sorceress for the deed in the person of King Arthur's magically-empowered sister, Fata Morgana.

The Arthurian legends had spread from Britain to all of Europe by the year 1000 A.D. The romantic Latins had their own versions to tell on firelit evenings and stories of the enchantress, Fata Morgana (Italian for Morgan le Fay or Morgan the Fairy) was their favorite. She it was, they whispered to eager-listening ears, passing from one generation to another, who created the exquisite scene appearing at various times over the Strait of Messina. It was a magic no one tried to reason with. They just enjoyed it. And many were the tales spun about its wondrous unfolding over countless years.

The Déli Báb mirage of Hungary shares a similar background history. A magnificent scene of breathless beauty has been seen from time to time, hovering over the "Puszta," the Great Plain of eastern Hungary, since the most ancient of times.

As in Italy, the peoples of the Hungarian plain believed they knew the reason for the magical vision. It was the work of a beautiful enchantress in their classical legend, Déli Báb. This maiden of magic had been the daughter of the king of the Adriatic but she was captured a long time ago by a Hungarian fisherman who brought her up out of the sea to live with him on the Great Plain. She was not happy there and wept bitter tears until she melted away with longing and became a shimmering body of water or a glimmering waterfall by some castle in the distant sky.

As with the Italians, the Hungarians treasure their enchanted scene. Since the most ancient of days, many things change with the years, but not the magic of Déli Báb. She continues to come back from time to time. Chiefly, it is said, at the hour of noon or sunset and never when it is cloudy or raining. Déli Báb does not like the rain. Only the golden rays of the sun hours.

There is nothing more hauntingly beautiful than the Puszta at every hour of the day, even without its vision in the sky. The Great Plain once covered a large part of Hungary. Its lush grazing lands were the country's pride and joy. Used exclusively for cattle and horse raising, ranchers spent their sun-drenched days tending fat-ribbed herds of cattle. In recent times, however, progress and town development, as well as more economical farming practices involving the construction of irrigation channels and drainage areas, have all reduced the Great Plain to a small region around the eastern border city, Debrecen.

But the land there is still wide and wild and beautiful with tips of lush growing things brushing the winds. Gazing out upon it, even to this day, one can feel the people of this land deserve the Déli

Báb. They have toiled with the wheat of the plain and turned the soils of its earth for long contented but arduous years. Déli Báb is their reward.

Hungarians today will tell you that it was surely the reward of Ivar Kiraly, a youth who lived near Debrecen in the early 1900's.

Ivar spent his young herdsman life on the Puszta tending horses on his father's ranch and, best of all, riding his own magnificent chestnut stallion across the never-ending plain. He named his horse, Tatra, after the high mountains of northern Hungary. Together, the two, muscle-rippling beast and white-cloaked boy, would be seen by fellow herdsmen galloping across the Great Plain for hour upon breathless hour.

"Where do you ride for, so hard and arrow-straight?" asked friends from time to time.

"I ride for Déli Báb!" he would shout as one hand gripped the reins and the other his round black hat with a wide brim.

Ivar's grandmother used to talk to him on quiet dark nights after Ivar had pounced into his deep-feathered bed.

"Why do you chase after Déli Báb, my grandson? She spreads her magic high above us for beauty and admiration. She does not mean mortals to enter her kingdom. You must not try. As we all know, though many have sought her, none has ever caught up to her. She has always vanished before anyone can reach her. No one ever will."

"I will," Ivar answered her simply. "Someday I will catch up!"

There are those in Hungary today who swear he did.

But Ivar was still nowhere near his catch in the year 1915 when he turned nineteen and had to leave his beloved Puszta for the fields of war. He joined the Hungarian cavalry so that he and his horse might not be separated. Together they rode into the battles of Italy. Attack after attack, the two fought with ardor until one fateful day when the great chestnut stallion fell under a direct hit and his young rider was riddled in the legs by machine gun fire.

Ivar Kiraly returned to his white-washed home on the Great Plain on a stretcher. He was badly crippled.

His grandmother stayed endlessly by his side, nursing him back to health. How different the boy was. His eyes were no longer kindled with sparks. They seemed to gaze expressionless out towards the far horizon of the Puszta.

She knew he was dreaming of the chase of all his young days. Searching for Déli Báb and the past.

"You must forget yesterday," his grandmother comforted with a thin veined hand on his shoulder. "There are so many tomorrows to think upon."

But Ivar would only look up for a brief moment with half a smile, then return to his far away dreaming once more.

Finally spring came to Hungary. By May of that war-torn year of 1917 Ivar was well enough to stretch out in the sun-filled courtyard in the daylight hours. And how good those hours were! He would take a deep breath of sweet Puszta air, redolent with late-blooming lilacs. It had been a cold spring but now the sun was pouring a kindlier warmth on the Great Plain and Ivar's father made a promise to the youth. As soon as his legs were strong enough, the boy would ride the stable's fastest and most beautiful horse, a great white stallion that was the envy of every herdsman of the Puszta.

With such a promise, Ivar's cheeks began to glow with a tint of bloom. Soon, he could move his slim legs, so long cold and still of joint. In only a matter of a few weeks the young man stood up and walked about the courtyard with eager steps.

Then it came. On a spring-easy morning with no one about but a few cackling geese stirring at his feet, Ivar's eyes caught the wondrous sight over the far away fields, Déli Báb! In shifting glows of lavender and pink with streaks of gold etching the forms, Ivar watched the magical scene unfold. Castles and bridges and white stone houses were outlined against a blue sky. People sauntered on winding pathways. A waterfall shimmered down a mossy hill while, slipping downwards through the shafts of warm sunlight, was a long flight of dazzling steps!

Déli Báb had waited for him! This time he would catch her! Once and for all, the young man would fly to the arms of Déli Báb.

With a strength he didn't know he possessed any more, Ivar Kiraly flew to the stable, swung a saddle on the great white horse, fastened the girth with excited hands and mounted.

Ah, what joy! Like the autumn gales of the Great Plain, Ivar and the white horse swept out of the stable and flew across the fields, the boy's linen shirt pulling outwards from the press of the wind.

On and on they flew. Ivar's grandmother caught sight of the dashing forms too late to shout out a protest. What was the use anyway? She sighed. The boy must have his chase. And he had earned it, she knew.

But, she learned before the day was out, it was not a hunt such as those of old. Ivar did not return that evening, breathless and large-eyed with happiness, as he always had. The distant plain remained void of the galloping form she had always awaited with such pleasure.

Her grandson never returned. She never saw him again.

Others declared that they had seen him, though.

"I saw him on his white horse, Grandmother, riding as though the angels were bearing him along. You couldn't have touched him with a whip lash!"

A few days after that, a group of herdsmen stopped at the farm for a drink of water from the well. When questioned, they nodded spiritedly to the old woman. Yes, they had seen such a youth go by, speeding like lightning on a white horse, his cream-colored shirt billowing out and the lasso circling over his head in the usual greeting of the herdsmen of the Plain.

One more person, a traveler passing through the area, reported he had seen a young man galloping into the setting sun.

Grandmother nodded sadly.

It was Ivar all right. He had made a dash for Déli

Báb. This time, he had won the chase. He had reached the shining steps of the heavens and was finally safely "home."

To most this may sound like a strange story. An impossible tale. But it is not unusual to the Hungarians of the Puszta who know so well their wildly beautiful mirage of the Plain.

Ivar Kiraly finally caught up. That's all. He was now in the mirage.

Ask a Hungarian, "Have you ever seen him there?" And he will answer you without a tremor of an eyelash.

"Of course, everybody has seen him!"

A beautiful legend, we murmur. Perhaps. But can we be *sure* the tale isn't true? Was not the mirage itself once a magic no one could explain?

Chapter Five

ESP could be a faculty we used to have and are losing, or one that we're only gradually evolving to.

Charles T. Tart, Ph.D.
Associate Professor of Psychology
University of California at Davis

ISLAND OF ESP

The Outer Hebrides off the coast of Scotland are as near to being "out of this world" as any group of islands on the face of the globe. In every sense of the word.

Hundreds of tiny islands rise to greet the ocean foam and fury. Less than a fifth of them have served as habitation. Those that could boast of habitation have remained nearly as remote in tradition and custom today as they were centuries ago.

Of this latter group, St. Kilda was long the best known, yet the least visited. Perhaps, because the villagers preferred it thus and commanded the very elements to keep it that way.

Whatever the reason, one thing was certain through the years, St. Kilda was an extraordinary place. Its people seemed to share a common "island psyche." They lived not only physically apart from their fellow beings on other shores, but apparently lived at times on an even remoter mental plane!

In a word, St. Kilda was an island of ESP.

And, as such, for centuries was regarded by outsiders with curiosity and awe. More than that. Real fear.

The ancient Celts called this sunset isle, "The Land Under the Waves," referring, scholars feel, to the dangers experienced by anyone trying to reach the place. It was also labeled by ancient people as "Over the Brink of the Western Sea."

Authorities state that the isle's Gaelic name was "Hirt," or "Irt," meaning "Death." Such a connotation probably explains why the name "Hirt" is taboo on some of the Hebrides Islands and is forbidden to be spoken by the Outer Isles fishermen when they are at sea. It is interesting, too, that for years, a popular threat to a naughty child in this area was, "Behave or I'll send you to Hirt (St. Kilda) on a cow's back!"

But in time, St. Kilda's "Over the Brink" character became softened with understanding. She was not an isle to be feared because she was different. She was, perhaps, a place of divine purpose. A place to be needed.

The Scottish Stewards of the seventeenth century who visited her periodically as part of their stewardship duties found her to be so, at any rate. They discovered an amazing thing during their periodic residences: any ailments they had had prior to their visits, would vanish once they arrived at St. Kilda. Not only did they feel the island increased their good health; it brought them good fortune and plenty as well. St. Kilda, they were sure, had magical qualities.

With such favor, St. Kilda took on a whole new

aura of grace. It became a custom among the Scottish Stewards, on their regular visits to the isle, to take along with them all those from their province who were sick or in woe of any kind. After a couple of months, these people went back home in perfect health and peace of mind.

St. Kilda was "in."

In the centuries that followed, the people of this isle were spoken of as being the most hospitable and kind residents in all of Scotland. If men had to be shipwrecked, they prayed it would be near St. Kilda. For unlike other isles who regarded wrecked treasure ships as a "gift from the sea," the islanders here saved men not goods.

One day a remarkable incident occurred that ingratiated the unusual isle to all seafaring men forever. A Captain Otter and his crew strained to save their ship and their lives in a perilous all night storm at sea. With each thundering crash of wave, the men felt certain the ship would be spun over and down into the depths forever.

Suddenly, at the height of the fury, the winds changed direction and Otter was able to guide the ship to a nearby island for safety. It was St. Kilda. The ship rode out the remaining rains in security.

The next morning the men went ashore and found a smiling populace modestly hailing them and wishing them well.

Before the captain could complete his story, the villagers told him they knew all about it. They had known a ship was in peril out at sea and had spent the night in their small island church—all of them

—praying to God to perform a miracle and save that ship. And He did.

In telling that story all through later years, Admiral Otter never failed to state that he and the crew firmly believed that the islanders' prayers were, indeed, responsible for his ship's miraculous survival that night.

It is no surprise, then, to find St. Kilda earned a new name, the "Island of Second Sight."

Numerous instances in which the villagers displayed this common "island psyche" that was capable of mass ESP have made their way into Hebrides history.

Isolated as the islanders were from the mainland, the problem of communication in the old days was one to be dealt with. Though the people learned to read and write, they found the skill of little use. There was only one annual visit of a steamer bearing goods, news and mail. So they devised a mail system of their own. They made a bag from a sheep's stomach, filled it with their letters, then attached the sheep's large white bladder. This made it floatable as well as clearly visible.

Being able to sense the right timing, with wind and wave, they knew just when to throw the bag into the sea so that it would sweep into a shipping lane and be picked up. The system, it is said, worked beautifully!

One of the most famous instances of island ESP occurred in 1901 when a ship put in at St. Kilda to inform the residents that Victoria, Queen of England, had just died.

When the captain went ashore, he was astonished to see the villagers all in black.

"Whom do you mourn?" he asked, thinking some much-loved islander had passed on.

With handkerchiefs pressed to their eyes, the women moaned softly and the men held their hats respectfully in hand.

"Why we mourn the death of Her Majesty, Queen Victoria!"

"How did you know?" asked the amazed captain.

"We saw it," answered one islander, "we saw it."

One incident of island telepathy caused so much consternation and disbelief, the mainlanders shook their heads and murmured the first uncomplimentary comments St. Kilda had heard in centuries.

It happened in the autumn of 1914. A British ship off the Outer Hebrides was radioed to alter its course and make a stop at St. Kilda. The islanders must be warned that Great Britain was at war with Germany.

The captain was scarcely able to make his way ashore, the crowd of people surrounded him so impetuously. Their flurry of heated questions and excited gestures nearly overwhelmed him. Before he could open his mouth, he was assailed with:

"Whom are we fighting?" "Why are we fighting?" "Is the war going ill for us?"

The captain stared back at the people in utter astonishment.

"Yes, we are at war. With Germany. But how did you know?"

"We see many things beyond the shores of our isle," explained a man at his elbow whose deep eyes, even now, were looking beyond the officer's into the distance.

A woman rubbed her arms as though swept by a sudden chill.

"We saw soldiers—our soldiers—fighting with guns and long knives attached to the barrels. We saw them fighting men in gray uniforms, but we didn't know who they were—what their country was."

"Aye," added an older woman, "we see it is going badly for us. Many of our soldiers are getting killed. Are we losing?"

The British officer clamped his jaws firmly together.

"It does not go well," he said with coldness.

He said no more but pushed his way back through the crowd and on to shipboard.

His report later to the British authorities was brief and denouncing.

"A German ship or ships, without doubt, are using the island of St. Kilda for a secret base."

When questioned about the basis of his assumption when no evidence to confirm it could be assembled, the captain would not relent.

"It must be so," he insisted. "How else could they have known? No other British ship had made a stop at that island in months. There was no way the islanders could have had such information. I refuse to believe they could have 'seen' it in any other way than through enemy information."

But the captain was wrong. There had been no

other ship at the island—friend or foe. They had witnessed the battle as they had "seen" so many occurrences in their long island history. Through their mass "second sight."

The British captain could not believe that. Perhaps many people today do not. But ask any Outer Islander and he will assure you it is true. Recently, a Scotsman said,

"Telepathic powers, you see, became well developed on many lonely islands, though St. Kilda seemed the most astute. North Rona and some of the others, it has been well attested, displayed similar powers. They had to, to keep from utter isolation. Now, on the whole, it is fading. Wireless came to them and now they can be saved the trouble. You know, psychic concentration is a lot of work. They no longer bother."

"Were there any remnants of 'Island ESP' in recent years on St. Kilda?" he was asked.

"Well, there was the strange St. Kilda Cold phenomenon," he offered.

"What was that?" he was pressed.

"There is a belief that whenever a ship came to St. Kilda a wave of mass nose-colds swept the island! Odd, isn't it? But it's true. A woman I know stopped at St. Kilda a few years back on a private yacht. The residents swarmed cordially on board. Everyone, islanders and visitors alike, were in perfect health. The next day, everyone had noses dripping with heavy colds!"

"Sounds like their collective island subconscious resented intrusion," was suggested to the Scotsman.

"An outward negative manifestation of an inward displeasure."

Perhaps, St. Kilda, in her heart, has always wanted to pull away from tremors of the mortal world. Today, she finally has. St. Kilda's last inhabitants were removed a few years ago. She is too remote for modern habitation. Serving now only as a bird sanctuary, St. Kilda is once again just the island, "Over the Brink of the Western Sea."

Chapter Six

Who knoweth the mysteries of the will, with its vigor?

Joseph Glanvill

NEMESIS OF THE NORTH ATLANTIC

Nowhere in the world is there a more subtly-dangerous area than the North Atlantic. In the environs of infamous Sable Island off of Nova Scotia the Far North reaches a zenith of treachery. There its freezing cold current joins the Gulf Stream and deflects those warm waters with a vim, creating a mass of changing flows and whirling eddies. Such a trap is death to the most stalwart of men and vessels. Centuries of shipwrecks in this awesome area have proved this and inspired the nick-name, "the Graveyard of the Atlantic."

It is a ghostly region. Everything in the environment seems to join in a conspiracy to make it so. Not a tree or shrub graces the sand spit which changes form with every storm. Sandy hills rise at one end, covering the bony remains of some unfortunate vessel and sweep clean the other, revealing long buried galleons of another era.

The island reclines on its ocean bed so lean and flat of form, on a cloudy day, it is impossible to distinguish sand from sea. Thus it lies in wait, surrounded with tentacles of inner, middle and outer shoals, to catch and claw and kill all unsuspecting vessels that come its way.

That catch, over the centuries, it is estimated, totals over five hundred ships and five thousand lives. A record that leaves in its wake a crew of ghostly inhabitants. Phantoms, ranging from a bleeding woman to a powerful life-saver who emerges to brave the white-capped crests every time there's a shipwreck, haunt the island. All echoes from the spirit world, it is said, recalling earthly tragedies.

But, perhaps, the icy waters as they stretch out far into the ocean carry the most ghostly forces with them, as subtle as the currents that flow unseen. Mysterious powers, it would seem, lie hidden in the North Atlantic as sure as icebergs conceal their bulk below the surface.

One familiar tale concerns a ship that vanished in the North Atlantic in 1881, not once but *twice!* Although the distressed vessel was never identified, the British ship that found her was called the *Ellen Austin*.

The English ship spotted the schooner drifting in an erratic course and bespoke her. When no answer was forthcoming, the British captain ordered a boarding party over. Although the men found everything in perfect order with ample supplies of food and water on board, the schooner was deserted.

The captain decided to salvage the abandoned ship, so he placed a prize crew aboard with orders to sail the ship to a common destination in Newfoundland. No sooner had the two ships started their course northwestward, than a heavy fog swept

79

over the sea and they disappeared from each other's sight.

Two days later, when the mists cleared, the British captain caught sight once again of the stranded schooner. It was not too distant, but as before, it was drifting aimlessly. Again, the English ship hove to, and once more, a boarding party was sent over by the captain. They, too, found the ship in perfect shape, but not a soul on board! There wasn't a thread or button left of the salvaging crew!

The British sailors hastened back to the *Ellen Austin*. Not a man among them would agree to stay on board the mysterious craft. The British vessel pulled away from the strange schooner and it was never seen again.

There is another sea story from this area even more intriguing. It occurred about a century ago.

A British ship headed on a course southwest, was ploughing through the Atlantic waters with nary a problem when a strange thing happened.

The first mate stepped into the captain's cabin and was surprised to find that his superior was not there but a man he had never seen before! The man was thin and tall and dressed in heavy winter garb. He looked from another planet; certainly from another ship! The hood to his jacket was coated with ice and his unshaven chin was shimmering with ice crystals. His eyes beneath shaggy frozen brows stared at the desk before him as he picked up a chalk piece and began writing on the captain's slate log. His white hand scrawled with difficulty on the gray stone surface.

The mate had paused in the doorway, his senses stunned. His presence didn't seem to attract the attention of the stranger at all. Then, feeling he was out of place, or at very least, seeing something he shouldn't, the mate backed up quickly and shut the cabin door behind him.

Had the captain brought some unscheduled passenger aboard? Why was he in such an ice-bound condition on such a fair weathered day? Who was he and why was he there? The officer thought it best to make no comment to anyone. He returned to his own cabin in silence, afraid somehow of what he'd seen.

In less than an hour, the captain ordered his mates and the crew on deck. He questioned them all with a scrutinizing gaze.

"I returned to my cabin, a short time ago and found someone had had the boldness and lack of discretion to write an order on my slate log, directing this vessel off course. Done without my consent or any prior discussion with me, I consider this an act of senseless and dangerous frivolity. Some member of my crew is either a fool or a criminal! I demand to know who is responsible for this message!"

The captain held aloft for all to see, his slate log. Scrawled across its surface were the distinct words:

"Steer to the northeast."

Not a man moved to step forward or make an acknowledgement of the deed. A flush seeped over the captain's face, slowly, in anger.

"I insist—"

The first mate stepped in front of the captain.

"You!" exclaimed the captain with rising indignation.

"No, sir, not I," answered the mate. Then he swallowed hard before continuing. "A passenger on board wrote it, sir, I saw him."

"A passenger!," exploded the captain. "What passenger? We have no voyagers on board nor any stowaways, I presume. Why speak you of a 'passenger'?"

"I only assumed the man was such, Captain, for he was not a seaman nor an officer nor anyone I had ever seen before. Thinking I had intruded where I should not have, I withdrew. But I did see this man, sir, in your cabin as he was writing on your log. He looked more like a resident of the North Pole than an Englishman. I had no idea what—"

"Search every keg and crate on board this vessel!", ordered the captain as he swung around. "I want to know who and where this stowaway is and have him brought to my cabin!"

Hours of searching by the crew brought to light not a single clue to the presence of any stowaway. There was no one of such a description on board.

The captain sat at his desk for a long period of time after that, He studied the sketchy words on his slate. Something about those four words was compelling. Who had written them? Why did they strike him now so forceably? Could someone have possibly written them in a state of sleepwalking? Hardly a likely solution. And even if someone had, what would be the reason behind such a strange command? Why shift directions to the coldest most dangerous course in the Atlantic? Why, he couldn't seriously consider such a thought. He was due at port with his cargo on a schedule tight enough as it was.

Yet—The captain got to his feet, stared out the glass across a smooth sea and pondered.

Was there a reason he received that message? Had he the right to ignore such a direct appeal? What was it that lay to the northeast?

He didn't know yet. But he was going to find out. He rammed on his coat and strode out to the pilot house.

"Steer to the northeast!," he commanded as he slammed the door of the pilot house behind him.

The surprised mate, with a quick, "Aye, aye, sir!" swung the wheel in a smooth arc and the vessel began to turn slowly northwards.

The captain stuck to the bridge until the bitter winds drew him periodically back to his cabin or to the pilot house.

Then it happened. Just before sunset, with icy floes sparkling in the setting rays all around them, the second mate sighted a waterlogged vessel drifting with the currents like a plank of dead wood.

"Vessel athwart!" called the mate, as the captain joined him at the rail, straining his eyes to catch sight of every detail. Within minutes, they had pulled abreast and a boarding party sent across. The stranded ship was manned by a near-dead crew of starving, ice-coated men. One by one, they were taken on board the British ship, their frozen mouths warmed with hot soup and their stiffened bodies encased in wool blankets. Crystals encrusted their hair, their eyebrows, their sea jackets. They looked like a crew from a phantom ship.

As the last man was carried on board, the first mate sucked in his breath in a quick gasp. It was he! The tall stranger he'd seen that morning in the captain's cabin, writing on the slate! He had on the same ice-coated jacket. His thin beard was covered with ice crystals. Even his shaggy brows. The pale hand that rested still by his side now was the very lean one that had scrawled with such effort on that slate log that morning!

The captain listened to the story from his first mate. The man he'd seen was the very one they'd just rescued!

"I believe you, sir," replied the captain. "I have no explanation but I do believe you. I know there must be strange forces at work in this world which we are not yet able to understand. Else how could I have known so well I must steer northeast no matter what? And thank the Lord I did. A score of men would have died, had we not."

Later, on the return voyage to port with their cargo of human lives, the captain asked his first mate and the tall man with the shaggy eyebrows into his cabin.

He handed the stranger the slate log and a piece of chalk.

"Would you be so kind as to write for me the words, 'Steer to the northeast' on my log?

The tall man looked puzzled. He hesitated, then reached for the slate. With a sweeping hand, he wrote the message.

The captain and the mate exchanged glances. It was the identical handwriting. Wide and sprawling. Unmistakable.

"Thank you sir," said the captain as he put the log down on his desk top. "What were you doing sir, as you awaited rescue?"

The tall man smiled. "Nothing much. Just closed my eyes and kept on knowing that somehow we would be saved. The other men didn't believe it. They had all given up. But I hadn't. Then yesterday morning, just before you arrived, I went into a deep sleep. Almost like a trance. And when I woke up, I was so happy. I really *knew* then, that we would be saved. I just *knew*."

The captain returned his smile.

"I think I knew it, too."

"How incidentally, did you think to steer out of course?," asked the stranger. "How did you know we were there?"

"You told me."

Then the whole story was given to the rescued man who could only shake his head in amazement.

Men who have listened to this tale over the many years since it happened have shaken their heads in wonder, too.

A marvelous tale of a time when a man's faith dispelled the old Nemesis of the North Atlantic.

Chapter Seven

There are some secrets which do not permit themselves to be told.

Edgar Allan Poe, *The Man of the Crowd*

MOUNTAIN OF MYSTERY

Around the year 1850 in a village of Burke County, North Carolina, a strange incident occurred that seems to have triggered a mystery that remains to this day.

One of the community's residents, a hard-working, down-to-earth sort of woman, without any reason any one could think of, simply vanished. She was seen about her chores as usual one day, then was gone without a trace, the next. Although the husband bemoaned her disappearance and made no effort to discourage searching parties, still, suspicion from the authorities and the neighbors rested squarely on the lone man. When bloodstains were found on the stile behind his house, such opinions became rock-fast.

"Why, those stains came from a pig I butchered a few days ago," protested the husband. "I carried it to my smoke house, passing through the stile on my way. I've done it a thousand times!"

Mayhap, thought the neighbors, but all the same, that man was level-calm for a husband who'd just lost his wife. And didn't she have a substantial pocket? Aye, there was good cause for him to get rid of her, no doubt about it.

Not many days after the disappearance, a farm laborer, who had done chores for the husband, was spotted driving his employer's new horse and wagon down the main road of the village and out. The cart was filled with all the worker's belongings.

"Where be you going with our friend's horse and wagon?" asked a neighbor as he shaded his eyes with one hand.

"Bought it, good neighbor. Naught wrong with that, be there? Bought it, right and proper." With that, the farm hand snapped his whip airily and clicked jauntily on down the road.

"Aye," commented the farmer when questioned later. "I sold my gear to him. Don't need nothing that big no more."

Hubbub hit the village tavern that night, for there wasn't a body in the hamlet that didn't know that an itinerant laborer had no coin sufficient to be buying such fine equipment.

" 'Twas pay for his deed!," pronounced one man between swallows of applejack.

"You mean, the helper did away with her?"

"Naught else," answered the first man with a bang of his fist on the pine table.

"Mayhap, our scheming friend did the dire deed himself," suggested a man across the room. "But his farm hand caught him in the act. He couldn't do away with two bodies, so he thought 'twould be best to bury one and buy off the other!"

The two tavern friends stared at the speaker for a moment, then nodded slowly, almost in unison.

"Aye," they agreed. "That is a likely truth."

Whatever the truth actually was, no one ever found out for sure. But there was damaging evidence that the woman had met with foul play from some direction. It was uncovered long years after the disappearance. A stack of human bones was found under a cliff on Brown Mountain, the geographic backbone of this North Carolina county. They were studied by medical examiners and pronounced unmistakably the skeletal remains of the long-missing woman.

Though her bones defied detection for numerous years, it would seem her spirit did not. Not if the local townsfolk of the day are to be believed.

It seems, right after the wife's sudden vanishing and the endless hours of searching by her fellow villagers that followed, a strange thing happened on Brown Mountain. First here, then there, when a man would lift his gaze, he'd see a flickering light that would bob and flicker, or move from side to side for long minutes, then fade away. One after the other, various searching parties reported the same phenomenon when they returned home.

Talk in the tavern and by the kitchen hearths soared with excitement after that. Not one of the townspeople denied being scared. "Who wouldn't be?" they exclaimed. "Those lights be the spirit of the dead woman coming back to haunt her murderer!"

Spirit or no spirit, one thing is sure: the storied

lights that hover over Brown Mountain from time to time are still in action. They are seen frequently today and they appear with surprising regularity, as they have for over a hundred years.

The eerie haunting ground for "spirit lights" is, as mountains go, not very impressive. Lying, roughly, at the foothills of the Blue Ridge line, it is only a little over two thousand feet in elevation. Its name is certainly humdrum and its physical makeup incorporates nothing so intriguing as spooky caves to explore or challenging cliffs to scale. It is just an oversized, plain-spoken hill.

But it does have fame.

The story of the "Brown Mountain Lights" has spread from coast to coast. People have traveled from far points of the United States to witness the phenomenon. Few go away disappointed, so reliable are the appearances of the ghostly glows.

Local experts are happy to give out helpful instructions. First, one must be sure the night is clear. The "spirit lights" do not like stormy or rainy weather or even an overcast sky. Nor do they come into existence after a long dry spell.

So, on a clear, calm night, around eight o'clock, they tell you, go to the most famous vantage point for the show, "Wiseman's View" on Highway 105 near Morganton. Then gaze in a southeast direction. Sure as crows caw and chickens peck, you'll see a light take shape and glow red and clear as a giant ruby-glass lamp. It will rise until it seems suspended in space over the mountain summit, then, swiftly as it appeared, it will disappear.

But don't go away. In a few minutes, you will see the light form anew. This time it will be at another place on the mountain. It will hover there and flicker eerily for a few minutes then dim and disappear —only to pop up elsewhere on the mountain in a fresh spot. So it will go, off and on, all through the night.

The glows do not seem to appear the same to everybody, you should be warned. Investigators have found that one witness describes the light as a yellow glow; another as a ball of fire. Still others as pale white like candlelight. One man said the phenomenon appeared to him as a bursting skyrocket. In some cases, the light remains stationary. In other instances, it is said to move about in different places.

So much for how the lights look.

As for what they are. Well, theories bounce all over the place as fascinating as the lights themselves.

First, of course, is the suggestion, will-o'-the-wisp. That's always first everywhere where lights are involved in the mystery. Here, the answer is definitely "no." Will-o'-the-wisp appears only over marshy areas. There are no such bogs on Brown Mountain. Nor can they be due to any phosphorous elements or rock formation containing pitch-blende ore, since geologists declare the mountain consists only of plain granite.

Electrical discharges during a storm? Can't be, for the lights never appear in bad weather. Nor is the height enough to include such a phenomenon as the passing of electricity from a cloud to a peak. Although one recent Brown Mountain investigator from Toronto, Canada, Malcolm Bessent, feels the lights *are* electrical, due not to storms but to atmospheric effects peculiar to the mountain. Its topography, he points out, is aligned with the main Appalachian jet stream tract, a fact which could cause the strange atmospheric phenomena. At any rate, his camera verified the lights. Bessent reported obtaining several good shots of the weird glows (proving to his satisfaction that they were definitely electrical in origin) when he spent several days on Brown Mountain in September of 1971.

There is another popular theory—a mirage. And we're back to that near-magical thing again! Cool air sweeps down the valley at night, forcing the warm daytime air to rise over Brown Mountain. The boundary between the two layers of differing density acts, as we have learned, as a mirror. In this case, that interface reflects the glimmer of the brighter stars.

A neat-packaged solution and yet no one to explain clearly how one light could be bright red and hang for quite a length of time with no other reflecting lights around. Or how star-reflection could give off a display described as "bursting skyrockets" or "balls of fire." Nor how the lights could appear so brilliantly just after sunset. Nor how they do more than hover, more frequently, bob "up and down" or "from side to side."

Perhaps, the most commonly conceived theory is that the glimmers are the reflection of automobile lights or the glare of a passing locomotive headlight. But none of this gets anything more than a look of disgust from oldtimers around the area. The "Brown Mountain Lights" were seen many years before any cars were invented or any railroad passed by. By the same token, in the olden days, they used to say the lights were hunters' lanterns. "Way up there where no game is to be found!," scoffed the townsfolk even then. Of course, today such an out-of-date solution has long since fallen by the wayside.

For years, geologists, physicists, State Wardens, and more than a few government commissions have made a study of this mountain of mystery. No truly satisfactory explanation has emerged.

To most of the folk who work, play and live out their lives near Brown Mountain there is nothing to be perplexed about at all. Divine power is the answer. As one oldtimer put it:

"If God could make Brown Mountain, could he not also make the lights?"

Chapter Eight

Are we in the United States perhaps a mortality-ridden society, programming our lives to a shorter existence?

Dr. Alexander Leaf,
Chief of Medical Services
Massachusetts General Hospital;
Professor, Harvard University
Medical School

LANDS OF LONGEVITY

Bright-eyed, vivacious Khfaf was beaming more than usual on a day in 1849 as she donned her embroidered peasant dress.

All through the Russian village of Kutol in Georgia's Abkhazia at the foot of the Caucasus Mountains that morning was filled with activity.

From the doorway of nearly every wooden cottage came the scents of roasting chicken and mutton; seasoned beef and goat, bursting with the spicy tang of green onions and garlic. Then too, there was the irresistible scent of sweetened cakes, brewing teas and mellow wines threading through the high mountain air.

All of which delighted 16 year old Khfaf, for it was a day to be long remembered. It was her wedding day.

And long-remembered that day has been! Today Khfaf Lasuria is still recollecting it with the same vivacious glint in her eyes! She says she is 142 years old. Investigation supports her claim.

She can recall to you such momentous occasions of her long life as the time her young husband (they'd been married four years) considered leaving her and going off to fight in the Crimean War in 1853!

But more eventful landmarks of passing time embedded themselves in her mind. Over a quarter of a century later, after the death of her husband in an epidemic, Khfaf married again. It was a time of turmoil for her country which was involved in a long war with Turkey. A war which didn't come to an end until 1878. She recalls those days well.

Khfaf gave birth to a son in her early fifties. He is about 87 years old now. Her husband died almost 30 years ago. She mourns his dying so young. He was only a little over a hundred!

This amazing woman, serene and content at her extremely advanced age, is now enjoying her latter life. In an interview conducted under the auspices of the National Geographic Society in 1972 Khfaf said she had been active as a tea picker until two years earlier. In the 1940's she was the local farm's fastest tea picker at an age already over 100!

But in another southern republic of the Soviet Union lies an even more remarkable story. It is to be found in Azerbaijan, a mountain area hugging the Caspian Sea.

The tale begins with a history-making hour in Russia's record of events. In September of 1812 Napoleon tore through the borders of Russia and cannoned his way to Moscow. A move that spelled his doom.

In just a little over a month he was forced to pull back from the flaming city and limp back eastwards. It was an agonizing retreat for the French Army with the Russians nipping at their heels and the cold eating at their hearts.

The historic event for over a century and a half has been a military debacle one reads about in a book.

But to one man on this globe, it is not a piece of world history but a personal recollection! An unforgettable part of his youth! Incredible as it seems, this man, Shirali Milimovs, recalls sitting wide-eyed at his father's knee listening with quickened pulse to the terrifying story of Napoleon's invasion of Russia. He was seven years old at the time.

All of which tells us that this fantastic man is now 170 years old. He's the world's oldest mortal. Although Shirali has no birth certificate, the Academy of Sciences of the USSR corroborated this centegenarian's dates through medical investigation and research into military records.

Shirali's wife of 102 years is no piker, either. She is 122 years old.

Like the others in Russia's southern republics, the Mislimovs keep active and thoroughly at peace with the world. Both work every day in their fruit orchard they planted over a hundred years ago. Shirali also keeps busy in his carpenter shop as well as tending his sheep. For recreation he rides horseback and takes long walks. Lean and marvelous of build, he eats sparingly, enjoys his flocks of grand and great grandchildren as well as a worry-free life of peace and accomplishment. He has worked for over 150 years and has never been sick a day in his life.

It's not easy for men of other regions to compete with such records as these Soviet senior citizens have scored. But there are two other areas on earth that are near-equal in wonder where longevity rates are just as marvel-filled.

One of those is in the western hemisphere—a remote village in the Andean mountains of South America's Ecuador called Vilcabamba. There one comes upon such virile centenarians as 125 year old Miguel Carpio.

Senor Carpio, fit and robust, sports tawny-toned hair and sun-browned skin that belie his long accumulation of years. His spirits, too, like those of his Russian counterparts, are vigorous and alert.

Still active farming his land, Miguel considers himself "taking it easy" as we would phrase it.

"In my youth," he could tell you, "I was really active. I was a hunter and spent long arduous days, climbing steep mountain sides tracking down quarry. I stopped that when I was 73."

Miguel Carpio is only one of a high percent of elderly in this tiny village who have been interviewed by researchers in gerontology, a study of aging that has received impetus in recent years in countries all over the world.

How can one account for the longevity of these high-mountain South American villagers?

Another Miguel has his theories. He is Dr. Miguel Salvador, president of Ecuador's Society of Cardiologists. "The people of Vilcabamba never worry about anything," he told a reporter recently. "They have no electric lights, no sanitation, no newspapers, no radio or TV. They know nothing of the outside world and don't care to find out. They are happy and at peace. That's their main secret of long life."

Yet a third "mount of youth" exists. Probably the most famous one. The world's actual "Lost Horizon" since it is considered the inspiration for the famous book by James Hilton. Like the other areas, it is also a high, isolated region. This is the land of Hunza in Pakistani-controlled Kashmir. There equally remarkable old people who really don't look, act or think of themselves as anything out of the ordinary, carry on rigorous activities in their daily rounds at ages of 100 to 140 and think nothing of it.

A writer for *Let's Live* magazine visited the Mir (short for "emir" meaning "king") of Hunza a few years ago and reported the same observations as previous investigators: Hunzakuts live, frequently, to anywhere from 110 to 125, and the Mir told her, "we are all physically active and keep working."

A few days before the interviewer's visit, the tiny kingdom had been steeped in elaborate celebrations for a great occasion: the marriage of the crown prince. The palace was busy as the mountain's famous bee hives with the coming of thousands of the Mir's subjects to pay homage. Garbed in their most festive dress of embroidered hats and colorful veils, the people of Hunza feasted, danced and sang for three days.

One of the chief performers in the wedding festivities who danced with stately but easy movements in his flowing wool robes, was Kabul Hayat. He was nearly 100 years old and appeared fit enough to be judged about 65.

Another Hunza researcher, Renee Taylor, tells a fascinating account of her visit there in her book, *Hunza Health Secrets.* She could scarcely believe her eyes when she saw a 140 year old man playing volley ball! A most interesting segment of her account is her interview with an eighty year old man who looked about fifty. He told her the Hunzakuts felt the keynote to life lies in growing, not aging. Aging, he felt, was due not to deterioration of the body but to thought . . . man's enthusiasm and will and faith to live. No one in Hunza, he assured her, ever talked of age or of being too old to do things.

What is the secret of all these remarkable "Lands of Longevity?"

No one knows exactly what answer these three areas hold. But scientists from many countries are studying these peoples with careful eye. They are taking a long look at their lands, their eating habits, their working routines and, perhaps, most important of all, their philosophies. It is noteworthy, that although diet for the people of Hunza and Vilcabamba is low in calorie intake and fats consumption, the Caucasus region goes against all beliefs about longevity. The Russians eat a great deal of fats and dairy products and in some cases, are actually obese.

Activity appears to be a contributing force in this miracle of century-plus living also. In all three regions, the people keep busy and are enormously productive in their work. Everyday chores on their farms, in their fields and for their households in such wild lands require rigorous labor.

The position of elderly people in these societies can be regarded as enormously significant, too, say the experts. The great grandparent generation is not looked upon as a burden but a blessing. They are the experienced ones. They are sought for their wisdom and guidance. In the family unit, the word of the elder is law. In the community government, their participation is frequently sought. Especially with the Hunzas, one finds the aged have traditionally served as the backbone of the legal process serving as judges in court.

In none of the three areas does one find a forced retirement age. The older members of a family or a village are expected to contribute their share of work. And they do. In fact, surveys show that when an aged person ceases to be an active member of a group, he dies quickly.

But what is most telling is the fact that all the people of these areas "think young." No doubt, time will prove this the single most important factor contributing to longevity. When one asks any one of these people what age they expect to live to, one rarely receives a figure under 100.

Perhaps one can sum up the miracle of these Lands of Longevity with a philosophical comment. The fountains of youth mankind has sought for ages have always seemed "just over the horizon." Perhaps they are not afar off at all, but locked within man's own concept of himself. The horizon of such a beautiful view is not a "Lost Horizon" at all. It can be found in our world today, a bow of promise, rimming the lands of Southern Russia, Vilcabamba and Hunza.

Chapter Nine

St. Louis, Missouri Territory
North America
April 10, 1818

To all the world:
*I declare the earth is hollow, and habitable
within; . . . I pledge my life in support of this
truth and am ready to explore the hollow, if
the world will support and aid me in the
undertaking.*

Circular distributed by John Cleve Symmes
Late Captain of the Infantry, Ohio

MAELSTROM AND THE ABYSS

The concept of an abyss lying deep in the heart of the earth which is entered from some remote body of water or cavern has fired man's thinking since earliest times. It played an important part in the mythology of the ancient Greeks and Romans and continued to affect the religious dogma of subsequent European religions.

But the idea was more than a religious concept to the great Flemish scientist, Gerhard Kremer, who lived in the sixteenth century. To him it was unquestionably a geographic location and on his many maps he so designated it.

Kremer was a mathematician, geographer and painstaking cartographer. His reputation as an expert seems to have prompted him to mark up his successes, not to his own name but its Latin counterpart, a nomen of classic force: Geradus Mercator.

Under the stamp, then, of "Mercator" the geographer defined one of the world's most widely-used charts, the first "projection map." It appeared in 1568 and has been more generally used than any other projection map for navigation ever since. It was also revolutionary for another reason. It gave credence to the popular theory that there was indeed a deep abyss within the netherlands of the earth.

On his maps Mercator detailed his concept by representing the oceans as four currents rushing by different mouths into the northern Polar Gulf where they become absorbed into the bowels of the earth.

Right in this Arctic region he pinpointed what was and still is the world's most violent whirlpool. He called it the "Maelstrom," a term he derived, no doubt, from the Dutch *malen* meaning "to grind" and *stroom*, "a stream." It is as "Maelstrom" most subsequent writers and romanticists have referred to the infamous whirlpool of the Norwegian Sea, though the Nordics themselves call it the "Moskenstrom."

But "Maelstrom" or "Moskenstrom," the vicious vortex located in the Lofoten Island group northwest of the mainland of Norway between the isles of Mosken and Moskenaes has always been and still is another word for "treachery."

About three quarters of a century after Mercator presented his theory to the world, the islanders of Lofoten suffered a fright that convinced them that the cartographer was indeed right. Some super-fantastic force was at work in the Maelstrom. They had proof.

On the morning of Sexagesima Sunday in 1645 the whirlpool heaved and thrashed and slammed about with such violence the roar from its shrieking throat reverberated to the heart of Mosken, shattering the villagers' homes and sending their stone walls crumbling to the ground.

Perhaps it was that awesome repercussion that triggered a study of the matter from one of Germany's most renowned scientists of the 17th century, Athanasius Kircher. This brilliant man was an archeologist, mathematician, biologist and physicist and possibly the first scientist to hold that disease and putrefaction were caused by the presence of invisible living bodies. Kircher's main interest, however, lay in the study of subterranean forces.

There was an invisible area of the earth, he contended. A deep abyss girdled the underworld which was entered by the center of the Maelstrom and from which an issuance existed at the Gulf of Bothnia. This gulf is still so named and is found at the northernmost part of the Baltic Sea between Finland and Sweden.

But is it an exit for some subterranean passage that opens a wide, sucking mouth to the air at the whirling pool of the Maelstrom?

Although the Nordics of yesteryear insisted it was and many today are still firmly convinced that such is a fact, scientists have emphatically declared such an abyss in a molten earth's interior with an entrance and exit is impossible. The terrible vortex of the Norwegian Sea is not a violent upheaving from a subterranean source of any kind but is due to the crashing of waves rising and falling at the flux of the tides. As the crisscrossing currents blast their waters against the ridges of rocks there, they catapult themselves into a cataract. The higher they heave, the deeper they fall, creating a whirlpool with a terrible suction. This action is the cause of the Maelstrom and nothing else.

Although it has chalked up a record of a violent past, the Maelstrom has another side. It borders the North's finest fishing area. Even though it is located in the cold Arctic region, the weather is tempered by the North Atlantic Drift and has beckoned invitingly to the fishermen of Norway for centuries. Of all the good fishing coves none seems to excel over the area of small eddies near the Moskenstrom. Fishermen have declared that more could be caught there in a single day than elsewhere in a full week.

But very few have dared risk the formidable foe of the vortex so close by, violently impassable for six hours at a stretch, simmering down to a peaceful calm for a mere fifteen minute interval between the thunderous whirling hours.

Who would wish to risk entrapment in that powerful whirling mass of water that roars and tears and sucks everything near its grasp for six murderous hours?

In the early 1800's three men did. Peter, Fredrik and Niels Arneson, three brothers who lived in a small fishing village on the west coast of Norway. To them the Moskenstrom was a challenge well worth considering. But a deadly challenge it would be, they well knew. There wasn't a Norwegian alive who didn't realize that the Moskenstrom was not only a violent whirlpool, it was one of the earth's most awesome and mysterious terrors. What lay beneath those jagged rocks and powerful currents that formed the terrible pool? The abyss. When the pool sucked, it drew men and ships and animals and houses and all that fell into its heart down, down, down, deep into a subterranean area that penetrated the globe right to the very bowels of the inner earth.

But abyss or no abyss, to the three ambitious Arneson brothers the Moskenstrom meant one thing: the finest fishing in the world if a man had nerve. Peter, Fredrik and Niels felt they had it. Plus the skill to put it to practical use. All a man need do was time himself, *exactly*. Fearsome as the vortex was with its roaring, smashing and plummeting, a man could make it across during the fifteen minutes of relaxation. That moment of tranquility was a supreme opportunity. Once across the becalmed area, a fisherman could haul in for himself in the eddies beyond a bigger catch with more varieties of fish than most fishing vessels could acquire in seven days! Then when the pool slackened again after six hours, cross back again.

One day the three brothers talked over the plan. They decided to do it the next day. Timing the moments of calm *to the very second*, the Arnesons sailed their schooner-rigged smack of about seventy tons out of its cove a few miles northwards, cut across the Moskenstrom, dropping anchor beside small eddies where they stayed flinging and hauling in their nets until slack-time had again come to the Moskenstrom. Then they sailed back across it during the fifteen minute calm and headed for home.

This success was more than they dreamed of. They set out again the next day. And the next. Week after week, month after month.

The venture proved profitable beyond their keenest long-term expectations. The Arneson family became the envy of the village from the point of view of their success. But not from the angle of nerve-fraying experiences. Not a villager envied them that, or wished to participate in one small fraction of such hair-raising adventure.

Peter, Fredrik and Niels only threw back their heads at their fellow fishermen's awe. There was nothing to it, if one had nerve and a cool head.

But even the cool heads of the three Arnesons had their hot moments. Like the two times the men couldn't get back across the Maelstrom in the slack-time. The wind they'd counted on which had taken them across it six hours earlier had died away and they found themselves faced with a dead calm. On those occasions they were forced to spend the night within eye and ear of the terrible whirlpool. Its roar and terrible sucking sounds were a nightmare to experience from such close proximity when the possibility that they might be drawn into it was ever present.

On another even more memorable night, the men were held to their outpost of sea on the far side of the vortex for a week because of the sudden arrival of a storm that made crossing the Moskenstrom too risky even at tranquility time. They nearly starved to death and would have been washed to their deaths in any case by the gale, had they not had the good fortune to drift into one of the many cross currents that carried them out of the danger zone.

But the harrowing tales they brought back to their friends centered chiefly around the vortex itself and their close escapes from being a minute or two behind or before the slack-time. On occasion, the wind would be a little less strong than they had calculated it to be for that day, bearing them back across the pool a minute or two later than they'd planned. Or the currents would run a bit slower than usual and, again, find them at the very edge of violence. It was at such incalculable moments that the terror chilled the three brothers to their bones and they would almost swear off the whole system, until they were safe at home by their hearths again and talk turned to the ever-mounting financial gains. At such moments, the risks seemed to diminish and the tingling excitement of it all reigned as the supreme emotion, flavored and enriched by the amount of coin that was filling their pockets.

So it was, in such ways, the Arneson fishermen ran the gauntlet of the Moskenstrom for over six years. Though there occurred many a fear-filled moment, there was never an actual mishap.

Then came the 20th of July in 1834. The annals of fishing tales and ship disasters contain no experience of man more terrifying.

The day dawned as serene and lightly breezy as any fisherman could have hoped for. The Arnesons weighed anchor as usual and glided out of their cove and down across the Moskenstrom's calm without a hitch. For the next few hours, they pulled and hauled until the deck lay heavy with a good catch. Peter checked his timepiece. It was seven o'clock. A smart wind arose and began to whip at their starboard quarter. In the next moment, they all looked up to see a frightening sight. A huge cloud the color of red dust was pitching at a terrible velocity across the heavens towards them. The men looked at each other. Hurricane! Their eyes told each what every man was thinking.

"Don't worry!" shouted Peter against the wind as he pointed to his watch. "Weigh anchor now and we'll be blown into the Moskenstrom at slack-time! Can't miss!" The other two nodded. Slack came at eight. They should be on a perfect schedule.

Peter was the chief calculator. He knew every rise and fall of tide; every ebb and flow of current. He had never missed the slack estimate by more than a minute in a storm crisis. And even then, they'd always made it.

The storm broke with a fury within seconds. It became so black the men could not see each other. The next thing Peter heard was a mast snapping and then the mainmast toppled, followed by a shriek from the youngest brother. Before Peter or Fredrik could lift a hand, Niels was swept overboard and vanished in the foam of the waters. The two remaining brothers were helpless to do a thing but cling desperately for their lives where and how they could.

Peter flattened himself on the deck, grasping a ring-bolt at the foot of the fore-mast. As the waters heaved and surged over his body, his brain tried to think clearly. The time was still good. There was nothing to fear if they could ride out the storm. Suddenly, he was encouraged. Overhead, the clouds broke apart and a brilliant moon pierced through.

In the next moment, Peter's blood froze in his veins. He caught a cry, one long agonizing scream from Fredrik that beat aginst his eardrums in the furious wind.

"Moskenstrom!"

He heard it. He heard it all too well and he felt his whole frame shake with fear. In spite of his good calculating, *would* they hit the pool at slack-time?

Aye, they must!

With dripping hands and numb fingers, Peter pulled out his timepiece and stared at it in the wan moonlight as the ship rose and fell in the giant swells.

His heart skipped a beat. His watch had run down at the hour of seven! How long past that hour had it been when they weighed anchor to head for home? No matter how much later, three minutes off—or even two—would mean they'd hit the vortex in full fury! Peter threw the watch into the water and shut his eyes in anguish.

The next thing he knew, the ship was rising as though pitched by a giant hand onto a mountain top; then, in the next instant, it was slipping downwards as though falling from that peak. In that moment they were high on the swell, Peter looked down to catch sight of a whirling mass of water less than a quarter of a mile away. The Moskenstrom!

They were headed straight for it!

Peter looked up to exchange glances with Fredrik who was at the stern holding fast to a large water cask which was lashed under the coop of the counter.

He nodded back at Peter with fear-filled eyes. They both knew what each was thinking. They were doomed.

Suddenly, the waves subsided and the boat was sent into a temporary calm before, without warning, it shot off into a new direction. At the same moment the wailing of the wind and the roar of the water changed into a shrill shrieking. Peter knew what that meant. They were hurtled onto the "dish" of the whirlpool, the upper rim of foam that always edged the vortex.

Then a strange thing happened. At the height of his fear, a sudden calm came over the man. This was it, he thought. Nothing could change that. He now thought he didn't want to. Of course, this was his end, but what a magnificent end! He was about to participate in one of the most wondrous forces in all of nature. He was going to see what few men were privileged to witness—the inside of the terrible vortex—the "eye" of the Maelstrom. And ultimately, he would see that great hidden mystery of the world . . . the earth's abyss! Was not all this a privilege worth dying for?

Peter wished fervently he could pass all this on to Fredrik. But it was impossible to communicate. The ship at this moment gave a sudden leap and swept swiftly over the rim of the "dish" into the Maelstrom itself. Peter felt as though his stomach had pushed up into his throat. It was like plummeting into a bottomless void.

Minutes later, Peter opened his eyes to look upon a most remarkable vision of frightening beauty. Caught about halfway down the sides of the vortex, the vessel seemed suspended at that point by the fantastic speed of the whirling. Around and around they sped. Peter glanced down with astonishing quietude. In the moonlight he could see the over-whelming walls of the Maelstrom rearing up around them on all sides. Beneath him in the churning depths, rested a magnificent rainbow, arching up-wards from the mists.

Gradually, Peter was able to make out details of the experience. They were not alone. The forms of other ships, battered and broken, whirled along beneath them. Also, numerous everyday objects such as tables and chairs and old water casks. As he watched, one by one, these objects were whirled lower and lower into the vortex until caught in the suction of the "eye" and pulled out of sight forever.

If he could just manage to live long enough to see it, what a sight that subterranean passage would be! What aged pieces of the past must have accumulat-ed in its bowels, sweeping through the underworld Gulf, far from man's sight and knowledge!

As he gazed, a new observation entered Peter's mind. Not *all* objects caught in the whirlpool were sucked into the depths! He observed that *one* type of object was not drawn down but remained whirl-ing and whirling—those things that were cylindrical in shape!

He then began to recall that along the shores of the islands, he had many times noticed the pieces cast back upwards by the Moskenstrom. They were always barrels!

His calculating mind went fiercely back to work. Was it possible that a cylindrical object when caught in a vortex offered more resistance to suction than another object of equal bulk but of another shape?

It must! With a burst of new-found energy, Peter in a swift moment, released his hold on the ring and made a lurch towards a water cask within reach. He was now convinced there was one way to lick the Maelstrom. He would cut loose the barrel from the counter and use the lashings to tie himself to the cask. With that he would throw the dice once and for all, leap into the waters and cast his fortune on his calculations. They might be the last he'd ever make, but he was going to make a final try to outwit the pool!

He called to Fredrik, who seemed utterly to refuse any suggestions. Frustrated, Peter then tried to signal his plan by pointing to the barrels that repeatedly whirled past; then showed his own act of tying himself to the empty water cask.

Fredrik shook his head vehemently. There was no time now to argue. Peter could feel the craft sweeping lower down the wall of the vortex. It was edging ever nearer to the deadly eye.

Peter threw himself into the whipping waters and prayed.

For about an hour he whirled with the waters. During that time he caught sight of his fishing craft with Fredrik still clinging, slipping lower and lower and lower until all sank completely into the bottom mists and was gone.

For what seemed an eternity, Peter went round and round until his mind was numb and near bereft of all reason and feeling. Finally, he opened his eyes to see what he could scarcely believe . . . the whirling was slowing up and the Maelstrom was beginning to flatten out. By slow degrees, the violence diminished and the bottom of the vortex was beginning to rise. Soon the wind was gone and he could see the moon setting over the island of Lofoten! He was finally, and at long last, floating on a calm pool of water right where the whirlpool had been! He was free! He was alive! Poor Niels and poor Fredrik were down beneath him forever a part of the Moskenstrom.

Six hours of hell had come and gone. Gently blown out of the Moskenstrom by a morning breeze, Peter soon found himself drifting in the fishing grounds of his friends. A vessel sighted him and he was picked up.

The breath felt gone from his lungs. His heart seemed to have ceased. Only his eyes would work as he looked up, speechless and paralyzed, at his rescuers.

Though longtime friends of his, not one of the fishermen recognized him. His black hair was white as the snow on the mountains of Norway. His face had changed from a brown-toned, husky-jowled man of the sea into a hollow-cheeked, wizened old man.

It was a long time before he could tell the story of his nightmare to any man. But he finally did. He lived and relived it innumerable times, telling it with horror filling his voice every time. To this day it stands as one of the world's greatest true adventure tales. Men still question the abyss but not the experience of Peter Arneson.

Many subsequent thinkers gave credence to the Arneson tale. It has been written up several times without a doubt of its veracity. This is not surprising. What is unusual is the amount of words written about the Abyss with equal air of factuality.

One such writer was Edgar Allen Poe. Before he ever heard of the Mercator theory with its Maelstrom, he stated, Poe wrote the vivid story of the "Ms Found in a Bottle" in the early 1830's. In this suspenseful recounting of a man's sea adventure, one feels somehow Poe was in tune with the old theories of Mercator and Kircher and others of past centuries. He certainly knew how to make a man "live" them, when he wrote the final paragraph to his story:

". . . the wind is still at our poop, and, as we carry a crowd of canvass, the ship is at times lifted bodily from out of the sea—Oh horror upon horror; the ice opens suddenly to the right, and to the left, and we are whirling dizzily, in immense concentric circles, round and round the borders of a gigantic amphitheater, the summit of whose walls is lost in the darkness and the distance. But . . . the circles rapidly grow small—we are plunging madly within the grasp of the whirlpool—and amid a roaring, and bellowing and thundering of ocean and tempest, the ship is quivering, oh God! and—going down."

According to Poe's own dating, this manuscript was written before Peter Arneson's adventure in the whirlpool of Norway and could not pertain to it or been inspired by it. Yet its similarity is intriguing.

After Peter's miraculous survival adventure renewing the Abyss concept, a whole new look at the Netherworld theory sprouted here and there. Jules

Verne used it to good advantage in his "Journey into the Center of the Earth."

It is interesting to note that two years after the Arneson incident Poe produced one of his most controversial pieces, the longest story he ever wrote, *The Narrative of Arthur Gordon Pym.* A wild sea yarn, the suspense writer based the first part on actual incidents, authentic sea adventures. But in the last part he branched out into a fantastic account of a journey to an antarctic continent peopled by strange creatures, primitive beings and prehistory animals, presenting the concept, readers were to deduce, that somewhere in the antarctic ice sheet a hole existed, leading into the center of the earth.

No doubt, without finishing the book which concluded with a superfantasy ending, Horace Greeley announced to the world in a stirring review, something to the effect that here was a *true* story that would rock the readership with its startling facts. In London the story was printed with the concluding passages omitted under the announcement that it was a factual account, also.

Such convictions haven't entirely died down to this day.

In the far West of the United States stories circulate among old wranglers and ranch hands of hidden subterranean cities deep within the earth, some related as personal experiences.

But back to that master of eerie tales, one of Poe's narratives was based completely on fact. The story he wrote in 1841 when he was living in Philadelphia and which he published in *Graham's Magazine,* of which he was editor. Just six years after the

Arneson incident, he wrote up Peter's horrible experience in the unforgettable, "A Descent into the Maelstrom." Though he mentioned no name or dates (he probably didn't know them), the facts are all there.

One wishes Poe had made a note as to where and how he heard the account. One can only surmise he either met Peter Arneson himself on some Philadelphia wharf or in some waterfront tavern or, more likely, got to talking to a seaman from some Norwegian freighter in port who passed the tale on to the ever-eager listener. In any case, Poe heard about the remarkable incident and immortalized it.

The world is not likely to forget the Maelstrom, Peter Arneson or the controversial Abyss, thanks to many a curious and investigative scientist and writer, among whom, fortunately, were such greats as Edgar Allan Poe and Jules Verne.

Chapter Ten

I am content with my knowledge that mystery does occur, although I may not know why.

Cicero, Essay of *Divination*

AREAS OF ASSAULT

From time to time and from place to place throughout history, man has been attacked by missiles from space of one kind or another. Such objects have varied from ever-popular rocks and stones to pebbles, nuts, bones, nails, pins, and even statuettes and more!

Such flying objects come heaving through the air, either indoors or out, from no visible agent and for no understandable reason. And, in nearly every case, though the attacks are frightening, they are harmless. Seldom has a victim ever been fatally hurt.

Reports of such supernormal attacks have been recorded for centuries in countries all over the world. One classic tale of the 1600's concerns a New Englander named George Walton who robbed and cheated an old widow neighbor and as a consequence suffered such an onslaught of stone and rocks raining down upon his house that he was forced to right his wrongs with the woman. The story has come down through folk-telling as "The Stone Throwing Witch."

"Mere lore," you may murmur. Perhaps so. But through recent years, long past the time of medieval superstition and witchcraft accusations, people of reason and intelligence have been reporting assault of such oddities as fish, toads, frogs, ice and even plastic! Falling right out of thin air, from no apparent source.

Another one of America's classic examples occurred in 1802 when an "epidemic assault" swept through the Berkshire Hills. It all began in a tailor's shop in Salisbury, Connecticut, at eleven o'clock on the night of November 2nd. The shop owner who lived overhead was awakened by a thunderous banging against his shop window below. He edged downstairs in complete consternation. By the light of his oil lamp he gazed at the besieged glass to behold large pieces of charcoal, chunks of mortar and large rocks come crashing through the window as though flung with a vengeance.

He peered cautiously outside but could see not a sight of a soul. The moon was full and brilliant and he could see the village street clearly. There was no one.

After a sleepless night, the tailor finally found peace with the rising of the sun. The bombardment ceased and never came again. He was lucky.

Ezekiel Landon who lived a short distance away was not so fortunate. Similar missiles rapped at his house for a full week, striking his wife and children till they were black and blue and smashing every pane of window glass. At no time could any of the family see anything coming towards the window until the glass shattered. Sometimes the flying objects of mortar and charcoal stopped abruptly as though dropped deliberately on the sill by some unseen hand. Soon the attacks hit other homes in Salisbury. For weeks, sticks and stones poured in through holes made in the various window panes as if aimed carefully by a gunner. The townspeople were terrorized for a month before the weird assaults stopped. It was a long time before the houses and their owners recovered from the whole disastrous affair.

Nearly 40 years later, the inexplicable occurred again—this time in the South of the United States . . . on the Tennessee farm of the E. M. Chandler family. Negro slaves were working in the tobacco field on an August afternoon in 1841 when suddenly they saw a red cloud moving towards them across a clear blue sky. It traveled rapidly from East to West and just as it came over their heads, something rained down upon them with a "plop."

The slaves thought, at first, it was hail. They shielded their heads until the dark clouds had passed; then peered upwards. It was clear once more. But as they looked, all around on the ground and on the tobacco leaves were tiny pieces of skin.

In abject terror the slaves ran to the plantation mansion where Mr. Chandler was sitting chatting with a friend, J. M. Peyton. "A rain of flesh!" echoed Chandler incredulously. He looked at Peyton and Peyton stared back at him. Shaking their heads, the two men stalked out to the tobacco field. They were nonplussed. It was as the slaves had said. Pieces of skin lay strewn all over, some about the size of a quarter; others as big as half dollars.

The incident received widespread attention in the town, Spring Creek, as well as in the press and the nearby "Halls of Learning."

The Chandler farm was soon deluged by unbelieving villagers, curious investigators and researching scientists. Among the latter was the well-known Dr. Gernard Troost of the University of Nashville whose experiments in geology and pharmacy had received international acknowledgement.

After thorough tests, Dr. Troost stated that the flesh was indeed "animal matter" and that it had originated on earth.

Speculations by scientists then ran rife throughout the United States. They were publicized in newspapers from coast to coast. The flesh was food dropped by a flock of buzzards; it was torn pieces of chicken skin swept by a wind current from a barn yard; it was bits of decomposing cow or pig picked up by a storm miles away and deposited on the tobacco field. . . .

Or, was it as some people suggested, the remains of a man from another planet whose space craft had crashed and sent his flesh flying back in tiny bits on a passing air current?

As always, the explanations were as titillating as the incidents themselves.

Five years later in 1846 in the township of St. Mary's, Illinois, two boys met as strange a fate as ever happened to any mortal. They were leaving the barn after finishing their last farm chores of the day and were plodding back to the house through deep drifts of snow when suddenly, out of nowhere, an avalanche of snowballs stormed about their heads.

The two boys, Groves and Kirk, stopped and looked about them, a difficult task in the face of the onslaught. The night had settled down so dark by now there was nothing visible beyond the shower of white missiles. They wondered how anyone else could see in the dark to manage such a perfect aim upon them!

The snowballs pelted unmercifully. Unlike the usual soft balls of white fluff, these were so hard-packed they struck on the boys' heads and shoulders as severely as hammer heads. The icy balls did not break on impact, but fell to the ground like rocks.

Bruised and beaten the two boys struggled back to the house. Furious at the attack, young Groves' father seized a lantern and ploughed out into the deep snow. The balls flew towards him in a rain of fury, but not a person or so much as an arm or a fist, could be seen in the light cast by the lantern.

Before dawn, farmer Groves and the two boys arose, got dressed and hurried out for a second investigation. There was enough light to make out the strangest sight the farm residents had ever seen: snowballs were rising out of the middle of the white-encrusted field that had not an imprint in it! The balls flew at them like a rain of bullets. Grabbing pitchforks from the barn the three ran towards the center of attack, piercing the snowballs furiously. Not one broke. Not until the sun arose, did the attack cease and it never occurred again. It didn't have to, to inflict tragedy in the community. Within a year young Kirk died as a result, it was said, of the beating he received from the "snowball attack-er."

In 1922, the town of Chico, California, was the setting of one of the world's most inexplicable happenings. It still challenges solution.

An area about the dimensions of a city block was suddenly pelted by a downpour of rocks. The stones were all oval in shape and weighed anywhere from an ounce to a pound. The deluge came straight down, not heaved from an angle or from any source anyone could determine.

For months the bizarre attack continued in defiance of every investigative measure. The local police scanned the neighboring blocks and searched every nearby building. They found nothing. The rock-rain fell in a direct drop from above in an area where there was absolutely nothing overhead but sky!

Guards were stationed about the "battle area" and kept constant watch. The rocks still fell. On one day, March 16th, the fall was unusually heavy and this time, the stones were hot! On another afternoon, the downpour was so severe it "splashed" onto the sidelines, splattering its missiles over the crowd of onlookers and injuring one person.

By now the press of the entire nation was carrying stories of the "Chico Miracle." Scientists from local universities came to the afflicted spot and did their best to come up with a plausible explanation. There was none forthcoming. One comment made by C. K. Studley, a professor from a nearby college was reported in the *San Francisco Examiner*: "The rocks, especially the larger ones, could not have been thrown by ordinary means."

What means did throw them?

No one has ever had an answer. As best summarized by the conclusion of the Chico Police Marshal after two months of intensive investigation: "I can find no one who can explain the matter, yet it did happen. Many times, I myself, heard and saw the stones fall . . ."

Then, suddenly as it had started, the "rain of rocks" ceased. Those months of attack are all but gone from memory, and have never occurred again —in Chico.

But they have been manifested again in other areas.

Take, for example, a print shop that was operated in 1939 near the Los Angeles City Hall. The strange assault in that store was thoroughly reported and photographed by the *Los Angeles Herald* of July 12 that same year. In this case, the shop owners, Mr. and Mrs. Harry Park, were astonished to find their place showered inside by falling nails, pieces of ceramic tile and even tiny little hand-crafted images!

Around the same time, the United Press reported an attack against the home of E. H. Burdette in Fresno, California. Not only did Burdette find his house pummeled by stones from out of nowhere, but huge walnuts and various lengths of bone! When the police came to investigate they were struck by the avalanche themselves.

No solution was forthcoming for any of these cases either.

The 1950's saw a lot of action from the "Invisible Ones."

In June of 1954 a rain of those ever-popular rocks put up a powerful showing for a family by the name of Bunch in Springfield, Illinois. The local paper carried the story with the usual amazement and curiosity. It seems that on the morning of June 25th, Victor Bunch heard a noise from the direction of his front porch. When he opened the door to investigate a rock flew past his shoulder and landed on his living room floor right next to the television set.

Mr. Bunch gave a startled groan just as his eleven year old son came flying towards him from the yard, yelling that a stone had hit him on the back of the head.

Victor Bunch shooed the boy inside the house and made a quick rounds of the house. There wasn't a sign of a soul. He crossed the field that ran back of his place, sure that he would spot a bunch of rowdy boys. There wasn't a creature in sight. As he stood staring about him, puzzled, another rock shot towards him and struck him severely on the back of the head.

Bunch lost no time calling the police. The officers made a thorough search of the house and the land. After some time the men came back to the home, shaking their heads.

"No one," they reported. Just then the two policemen looked upwards. A rain of stones was descending from the roof in a steady downpour! There was no one on or near the roof!

By nine o'clock that night, the mystery doubled.

Rocks began falling inside the Bunch house! Again the police arrived.

They couldn't believe their eyes. Rocks were falling from the ceiling! One of them struck a light fixture right next to where one of the policemen was standing. It made a resounding "ping!"

The officers searched the attic upstairs and every room in the house. They couldn't find so much as a hole in a wall or in any of the window screens. Nothing could have been propelled into the inside of the house from the outside.

Yet the rocks still fell from an invisible source. There was nothing unearthly about their composition. Under tests they proved to be regular Ozark rocks.

The town officials finally had to give up on the Bunch house phenomenon. They could find no physical cause for the attack.

One of the most unusual "mystery falls" that has occurred from time to time over the years and over the world, is that which has been dubbed, "angel hair." A silky, sometimes sticky, web-like substance has hit certain areas like a plague. For one example, on October 4th, 1957 (the same day, coincidently that Russia launched its first sputnik) from the skies over Ichinoseki City in Northeast Japan, fell a shower of "angel hair." A delicate substance made up of spiderweb-like threads showered down profusely all over the city from ten o'clock in the morning until noon. Scientifically analyzed, it was reported that the material was organic but definitely not webs or vegetable fibres. It was inflammable and dissoluble in hydrochloric acid. All of which gave no answer to the problem.

In this country, the center of "angel hair rainfall" seems to be New Mexico. No one knows *why* any more than they know *what*.

A particularly fascinating "web-fall" was a shower that took place over New Mexico on February 21st, 1958. It had all the shining resplendency of a fairy-tale incident. Glimmering threads drifted down over the town of Los Lunas decorating trees, electric wires, telephone lines, television aerials and even clothing of passersby with its silvery substance. A little late for Christmas, the town was, nevertheless, highlighted with glittering tinsel! No one ever discovered what caused the remarkable rain.

Ice falls are almost as popular as stones and rocks when it comes to paranormal precipitation. Fairly frequently reported, particularly over the United States, they fall heir most easily to explanation. Aircraft, it is usually adjudged, flying overhead are responsible.

Planes were considered the explanation by most scientists of a "yellow ice fall" that hit the back yard and porch roof of J. L. Fitzpatrick in Warminster, Pennsylvania, on several different days during January of '73. Examined by chemists, physicists and various scientists of the area the weird pieces which were shaped like "flattened potatoes" were found to contain, like water from an old pipe, iron and magnesium. The yellow color was due to the presence of good old-fashioned rust. No doubt the fall had a simple solution: a plane coming in for a landing at nearby Johnsville Naval Air Station lowered its landing gear, an action which likely broke loose icicles that had formed there much as they do under automobile fenders when driving through freezing slush. These loosened pieces of ice then hit the Fitzpatrick yard.

Such an explanation is less than satisfactory to many science-fiction minded residents of the area. How could several planes passing overhead on different days all be responsible for releasing ice falls so perfectly aimed at one single small backyard below?

Such investigators preferring an extra-terrestrial answer, point out an interesting fact. On the first night the curious ice fell on the Fitzpatrick place, a strange yellow beam of light in the skies was spotted by some residents of Newtown hovering over the Southhampton-Warminster area southwards. Could the peculiar light have been related to the ice fall? Many townspeople of the region feel that it was.

Sometimes the "frozen rain" is meteoric in character. Such an example occurred in Richmond Heights near Cleveland, Ohio, in July of 1972. That precipitation accompanied by the sound of an explosion, created a crater some ten inches deep and about the size of a tire in circumference. Police Sergeant Martin Laro had an explanation for this phenomenon. It was not related to a fall at all. There had been an "explosion" just under the ground at that spot due to some kind of "chemical reaction." The ice had formed on the spot in its aftermath.

Even more odd than ice falls are repeated reports from all over the globe describing showers of toads, frogs and fish! An early example of such peculiar pelting occurred over Beaver County, Oklahoma, in October of 1912. A rainstorm broke just as a mail carrier named William Barthlot was going his delivery rounds in a horse-drawn wagon. Along with the sudden downpour of rain came hundreds of thousands of tiny toads!

Barthlot stared unbelieving at the tiny creatures collecting in his lap, on the wagon seat and all over the roadway. Each toad was miniscule, no more than an inch in length!

The mail carrier drove his cart back at a fast clip to town. Wide-eyed, he rattled into postal headquarters with the strangest "catch" he'd ever heard of. Scientists examining the miniature toads were completely flabbergasted. They had never seen such a tiny species.

Then there is the well-known annual fall of sardines over Yoro, Honduras, in Central America. Every year at the beginning of the rainy seasons, thousands of the tasty fish fall from the skies with no solution to "why?" ever given yet. The natives don't need explanations. They need only baskets at such times. The villagers prepare for the "gift from Heaven" well in advance. They gather every available basket, bucket and tub in the village, then assemble to wait in joyous anticipation. Since their village is way inland from the coast, separated by a mountain range, the free fish are a welcome delicacy. The "catch" it is reported, is always a windfall.

Texas who reacts big to everything as a rule,

thinks small when it comes to "fish fall." At least, Dallas did on June 18, 1958. On that day a shower of little fish pelted an area of that city for some time causing mouths to open in amazement. One wonders how many people inadvertently swallowed fish that day? Whole, uncooked and fresh from the sky!

Such falls of fish, frogs and toads are easy mysteries for the scientists of this world. They are due to powerful winds with vacuum centers like the "eye" of a hurricane. These forces "suck up" a load of small creatures and carry them for many miles before dropping them to the ground below. Sometimes the creatures they apparently carry are not so small. Mrs. Victor Mietans of Saginaw, Michigan, can testify to that. On September 7, 1960, as she left her house to go to market, she was hit on the head by a large perch!

No "rain," however, has been stranger than that which descended over Eastern Klickitat County in the state of Washington over a period of *two months*! It happened during September and October of 1957. What was the substance that fell? Plastic!

No one can explain satisfactorily as yet, why or how it happened, but they do know *what* it was. Over an area of many square miles the reports poured in describing falling pieces of plastic material. Some were sheets big enough to cover a bale of hay. The fall was of some balloon material, said the experts. If they were, the balloons must have been of enormous size and number. The amount of plastic that fell over an area about two miles in

136

width and 15 miles in length was almost immeasurable. Residents of that Washington county are still puzzling over the mystery to this day.

Not so strange of substance but just as problematical are the incidents of "localized" rain fall. The cases are small areas of precipitation. One such example occurred around the home of a Mrs. R. Babington of Alexandria, Louisiana, on the afternoon of November 11, 1958.

It was noon when Mrs. Babington drove up into her driveway and was stunned to see, although it was a sunny cloudless day, a small area of rainfall just before her eyes. Close to her house in a patch which measured roughly 100 square feet, it was raining a soft, pitter-pattering shower. Clearly visible, the substance could be seen descending like delicate needles.

Within minutes neighbors were over, witnessing the same event. Before long the town officials were present and the ever-ready newspaper men, one of them the managing editor of the *Alexandria Daily Town Talk*. All solutions were soon exhausted. The rain came from a little over tree top height. It was determined it could not have been from any local air conditioner or heater. Officials at nearby England Air Force Base said it could not be caused by any aircraft because of the size of the area and the time it occurred. Jets would have flown by such a small area in less than a second and though a balloon using water ballast could cause a mist after jettisoning some of its water, no balloons were in that area at that time.

The rain was definitely water. Newsmen present

felt it on their faces and heard it pattering on the leaves of nearby trees, though the back side of the trees, out of the rainfall area, were dry!

Mrs. Babington never found an answer.

A most unusual attack in the annals of mysterious happenings centers on the little village of Llano, New Mexico, lying in the green Santa Barbara Valley of the Sangre de Cristo Mountains between Santa Fe and Taos. It underwent a phenomenon in 1966. The rocks again.

One night in mid-July, Mrs. Jane Quintana ran out of her house screaming for help. Her husband, Alfares, looked about him in silent shock while the children huddled inside in complete bewilderment.

"Someone is throwing rocks at our house!" shouted Mrs. Quintana. The neighbors hurried to her aid and in no time, the local police had arrived. The rocks continued to shower down on the adobe house, clanked loudly against the tin roof and occasionally smashed through a window.

For weeks, the attacks continued every night, commencing sometimes as early as 4:30 in the afternoon. But even by daylight there was never any assailant visible. Soon, not only the local police were in on the affair, but the state police also. Day after day, night after night the officers and townsfolk kept watch. Still the rocks fell. Equipped with searchlights and guns, the men scoured every inch of ground. At one point they all shot a round of rifle fire in the direction from which the rocks were being thrown. Nothing happened. They could find not a trace of anyone.

Examining the farm set-up, the attack seemed

impossible. The adobe house itself sat high on a slope over the valley. The structure was surrounded by wide reaches of ground. There was no spot of concealment from which anyone could operate unseen.

Eventually, the stone-throwing ceased. Without any solution to the strange occurrence, the local and state police dispersed; the townspeople returned to their own kitchen-table talk; the Quintanas boarded up their smashed windows and went on living.

Another unsolved mystery.

England joined the list of "invisible attack" victims with a humdinger of a case which lasted for three years . . . from 1951 through 1953, at which time it all slowly came to a halt.

It involved an area of roadway covering a stretch between Cobham and Esher in southern England, which came to be known as "Missile Mile." A "land and air" attack similar to the Bermuda Triangle phenomenon, slowly unfolded. Motorists traveling the highway began to complain of being shot at by a sniper. They pointed to their pierced window shields as proof. Although what looked clearly like bullet holes were plain to be seen, there was never any sign of bullets or missiles of any kind inside the cars! Nor were there visible any second holes where the bullets might have passed out of the cars. The "shots" could not have come from passing vehicles as the victims were always alone on the highway. There could have been no hiding place for snipers. The "shots" occurred both at night and in broad daylight. Since nothing could be uncovered the police decided to patrol the area themselves in unmarked cars. On different occasions, two of these vehicles received shattered windshields. And they were no nearer a solution.

Compounding the mystery, aircraft flying over that area frequently experienced shattered glass!

The phenomenon gradually died down in 1954 and by 1955 ceased altogether.

But the speculating has not ceased.

What caused the mysterious attacks in that area between Cobham and Esher? The solutions offered by the press, radio, television and interested listeners varied from tiny meteorites to mad scientists' invisible rays.

The Automobile Association of Great Britain is to the point with its answers. The three or four year epidemic was due to either stress by ill-fitting glass; frame distortion; inequality of road surface setting up vibrations; changes of temperature or sound waves caused by passing vehicles.

Collectors of phenomena incidents find these unsatisfying solutions. To be the answers the glass of vehicles would have had to be generally ill-fitted for a three to four year period, then quite suddenly be generally well-fitted and the temperature changes must have suddenly become stabilized as well as the inequalities of road surface leveled off equally abruptly. As for sound waves from passing vehicles, it was clearly pointed out the cases of attack occurred when the car was alone on the road.

Also, there is the factor of how could all these conditions have affected aircraft?

In discussing this some investigators have offered, as in the baffling Bermuda Triangle, the possibility that, for a time, the highway became an area in which the known laws of nature ceased to operate.

But rest from all such outward assault in that area of southern England, as elsewhere, may be only temporary. As always with "Invisible Attackers" we are left with little by way of answers and even less by way of comfort. It is disquieting, to say the least, to feel at any time one might be a victim of such relentless warfare.

As we have seen, suggestions for a cause have varied from invisible men from Outer Space to laws of nature set aside for a time.

There is another answer offered by parapsychologists. Unexplained physical attacks in their eyes, generally fall into the category of "poltergeist activity." "Poltergeist" meaning in German, "a mischievous spirit" has been thought for centuries to be a disturbance due to mean, capricious spirits. Today parapsychologists declare that the physical phenomenon of material objects being thrown or heaved about is the result of the literally explosive nature of deeply repressed or frustrated thought in the subconscious of an individual or individuals which strikes out and orders matter into motion. Instances of mind-over-matter.

If this is so, then, perhaps, we will all have to be mentally at peace with ourselves and others before the world around us can reflect that stillness of living. Then, and only then, will all the world's areas of assault be laid to rest.

Why should we not hope and expect this to be so?

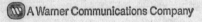

MORE BESTSELLERS FROM WARNER BOOKS!